2

The
Death
Mage

Densuke
Illustrations by **Ban!**

SUMMARY

Hiroto Amamiya died during a school trip and was reborn into a second life at the behest of the Reincarnation God Rodocolte. Due to a mistake by the god, however, he was born into nothing but suffering and eventual death. When he returned to Rodocolte, the god was concerned by the desire for vengeance he saw in the youth, and sent him to be reborn in a third world, Ramda, without any further powers. There Hiroto started his third life as the dhampir Vandal.

While suffering under curses from Rodocolte, Vandal still found a measure of happiness living with his mother Dalshia. When his mom failed to return home one day, Vandal used the death attribute magic that he acquired in his second life to create some undead and go looking for her.

Vandal's search for Dalshia brought him to the town of Evbejia, but he was already too late. His mom had already been tortured and killed. Vandal found her as a ghost, about to vanish completely. He placed her spirit into a remaining fragment of her bone and promised to one day obtain a new body for her. He also swore vengeance on high priest Goldan and the others who killed his mom.

After meeting new allies, enhancing his undead, and taking his revenge on Evbejia, Vandal and his party took to the road. They eventually encountered the ghoul elder Zadilis and saved her from an attack by adventurers. They entered a demon barren in order to get Zadilis home and found themselves unexpectedly welcome in the ghouls' grotto. Vandal settled down in the grotto for a while in order to train, and then made a big contribution by helping to defeat the Kobolt King Gyahn, who attacked with designs on expanding his own kingdom.

VANDAL

Hiroto Amamiya after his second rebirth. Born from a vampire father and a dark elf mother, he possesses massive magical power and command of death attribute magic. He is currently toiling under the instruction of Zadilis, chief of the Ghoul Grotto, in order to master non-attribute magic.

DALSHIA

Vandal's mother. She suffered a terrible death, but Vandal used his death attribute magic to bind her to one of her own bones, keeping her in the world as a spirit.

ZADILIS

The elder of the Ghoul Grotto. She appears to be a young woman but is 290 years old. Perhaps held back by her physical appearance, her mental age is not as advanced as her years.

BASDIA

Zadilis's daughter. A female warrior with an athletic, honed frame that also features feminine curves. She has taken a liking to Vandal.

VIGARO

The next chief of the Ghoul Grotto. Trusted implicitly by the young male ghouls and adored by the females, he's a ghoul with everything going for him. He is also Basdia's father.

SAM

A Ghost Carriage. Originally a servant killed by bandits and left to wander as a ghost. After Vandal avenged his death, Sam chose him as his new master and swore loyalty to him.

SARIA & RITA

Sam's daughters, who are also spirits. They received living armor found in a dungeon treasure room as their bodies, and look to be nothing more than empty armor.

CONTENTS

The Death Mage

Written by Densuke Illustration by BAN!

The Death Mage

CHAPTER ONE
GHOUL INFERTILITY ISSUES

Vandal was reborn into this world as a half-vampire, half dark elf dhampir. He was traveling with the spirit of his mother Dalshia, who had been executed as a witch, and a band of other companions.

During his travels he saved the Ghoul Mage Zadilis, which led to him learning magic from her at her ghoul grotto. After the celebrations for defeating their most recent enemies, led by the Kobolt King Gyahn, he continued to study magic under Zadilis.

But on that day, his normal passion for his studies seemed to be lacking.

"What's the issue, boy? Is there something stuck to my face?"

Zadilis noticed Vandal looking at her intently.

"No. That's not it," Vandal replied, shaking his head but still looking uncomfortable. The issue was, he really was seeing something on her face. *The specter of her death.* Vandal's eyes could see Zadilis's impending demise filling her smiling face. It wasn't going to happen in this exact moment, but it could happen in the next few days. He could be sure she wouldn't be around to see his second birthday.

Ghouls lived for around 300 years, so it was a little early, but not an unreasonably fast departure. In fact, considering the harsh realities of life in the demon barrens, she was doing pretty well. She didn't have any confirmed grandchildren yet, perhaps, but she had done well for herself. It would be the natural course of events to quietly watch over her peaceful departure from this life.

"Zadilis, do you think the two of us could have some time alone?" Vandal asked.

But sometimes, Vandal didn't want to leave things to nature. He would have liked to level up his skills a little more before taking on the very laws of existence, but he didn't seem to have the time for that. He had apparently surprised her so much he shortened her life, not so long ago, so he needed to take some responsibility for that too.

"The two of us—alone?" Zadilis widened her eyes at the sudden request.

"Yes. For something very important."

At his terse, abrupt tone, Zadilis thought maybe Vandal wanted to end his training and hit the road again. He had told her that his original plan was to reach Olbaum, a country beyond the mountains to the east of this demon barren. But she hadn't yet taught him everything about non-attribute magic control or alchemy. She wasn't asking him to settle down here for the rest of his life, but she did want him to stay for longer.

"Very well. We can talk in my house." Zadilis picked Vandal up and headed toward her home, hoping she would be able to somehow persuade him to stay.

"I can walk for myself," Vandal protested. "I'm almost two years old now."

"What you mean is, you aren't even two years old, boy. You tripped over just the other day," Zadilis replied.

At nearly two, Vandal probably considered himself close to an adult, but those around him saw a baby on the way to being a child.

They entered Zadilis's sunken dwelling, where she often trained with Vandal. The alchemy tools she had created for herself and a crystal ball were on prominent display. If there had been a bubbling cauldron in the middle, it would have been the perfect home for a fairy-tale witch, but she hadn't taken the décor quite that far.

"Hey, boy. If possible, I'd like to teach you all of the magic I know," Zadilis said, with a serious look on her face, after sitting down. This wasn't due to wanting to repay the child who had saved her life, or in thanks for contributing to the village. She simply wanted to help him achieve his full potential. "Boy, you don't have 'skills' in the normal sense of the word. You already understand that you aren't the quickest learner," Zadilis continued. "But you also have the right spark and instincts to cover those insufficiencies."

The instincts she was talking about were informed by the pop culture knowledge Vandal had acquired on Earth, the information he had absorbed from the spirits on Origin, and the imagination that they engendered. Vandal, aware of these contextual factors, wouldn't have considered them special instincts, or anything worthy of praise at all.

"Most of all, though, you have that crazy volume of magical power. You'll become a magician far beyond me, and in far less than one hundred years."

Massive magical power wasn't enough to make a powerful magician, but volume of magical power still mattered. The level of the skills in this world increased with use. That meant having the magical power to use spells repeatedly in rapid succession was vital to increasing magical ability.

In the case of humans, taking a magician-type job would also provide some vital modifiers, but the level conditions would have to be reached first before one could make the change. That was why humans and monsters who wanted to become magicians had to learn the fundamentals of magic and then increase their own magical power. In the case of monsters, most of them would give up rather than put the work in, or get killed before they could complete such training, so they often ended up falling back on whatever talents they were born with.

On that account, Vandal was blessed. He was free from the need for such training to enhance his magical power. Even without training, his MP continued to increase. He had over one hundred million and he wasn't even two years old. If he survived for long enough, he could potentially add tens of millions more to that number—even another hundred million. So his issues with learning could be mitigated by his innate skills.

That was what Zadilis had her eye on. She wasn't thinking of him as her successor, but as something far beyond even that.

"That's why I want more time with you. I know you have a purpose in your travels, but can you give me that time?" Zadilis asked.

"Yes. Leave it to me," Vandal immediately answered.

"Ah! Yes! You would?" His choice of words puzzled her a little, but the immediacy of his response pleased Zadilis. When he continued, however, she realized that there had been some sort of misunderstanding.

"I'll start the procedure at once," Vandal said. "Lie down and relax."

"The—procedure?" Zadilis asked.

"Yes. Leave it to me," Vandal said again, looking ready to get started with something.

He had seen the specter of death on Zadilis's face, due to the proclivities of his death attribute magic. He had therefore decided to try and extend her life. And he had assumed that the biggest obstacle to that would be Zadilis's own will.

Vandal had heard Zadilis talk about not having much time left, or having a successor, since he first met her. She also acted as though she didn't care much about living. He was therefore worried that she might reject attempts to increase her lifespan. But now she had asked him specifically to "give her more time." If she had said "let's leave things to my lifespan" or "going naturally would be best," it might have been different—or if she hadn't even believed Vandal when he told her she was about to die—but none of that happened. From Vandal's perspective, Zadilis had not only sensed her impending death but requested that he help her overcome it. Vandal was moved by her choosing to rely on him. He was almost tearing up, feeling such joy at having someone believe in him.

Of course, it was all just a misunderstanding.

"This is something required for you to learn from me?" Zadilis asked.

"Yes. A path that we must take," Vandal confirmed. If she was dead in a few days, or a month at most, he wasn't going to learn anything from her. Extending her life was vital.

"Okay. What are you going to do?" Zadilis asked, lying down on her back.

It reminded Vandal of when they first met. Remembering that he had been trying to save her then too, Vandal replied, "I'm going to make you a little younger."

"What? Younger? That can't even be possible—" she started to exclaim, and then gasped as a strange feeling swept over her while Vandal's hands pressed down into her stomach. Her eyes opened wide in surprise, and her lungs clenched at the overwhelmingly bizarre feeling of cold hands coming into direct contact with her organs.

"I'm using Spirit Bodification on my arms to directly inspect the condition of your body. It might be a little uncomfortable, but try to hang in there," Vandal told her.

The look on Zadilis's clammy face suggested that was a tall order, but Vandal was too focused to notice. This was actually his first time using Spirit Bodification to examine the body of another for himself, and he had no idea exactly what it would feel like for his subject. He knew what he was doing, however, like a skilled and practiced surgeon.

When he was being controlled by the researchers on Origin, he had been directed to use Spirit Bodification to examine all sorts of different things. Everything and anything from other test subjects—more poor souls like himself—to nuclear material in a lead-lined case, time and again. The Spirit Bodification magic items created from the MP extracted from Vandal had allowed Origin medicine and science to make leaps and bounds forward.

Putting all that aside, he had to focus on Zadilis's body. With his Spirit Bodification arms still inserted inside her—his arms that, in that moment, no longer physically existed—he then imagined them turning into liquid and flowing with her blood through to every part of her body. His arms proceeded to do exactly as he pictured. His Spirit Body was directly connected to his mind, making this procedure possible with Spirit Bodification.

This feels easier than it did on Origin, Vandal thought. *Is that just because I'm more mentally capable now? Or is this the difference with being in control myself?* Vandal was a little concerned with how easy it was, but he didn't have time to worry about that either. Zadilis was still gasping and groaning beneath him, clearly suffering. He needed to finish the procedure as quickly as possible, so he forced himself to focus on that.

Blood, blood vessels, brain, heart, nerves, stomach, liver, kidneys, pancreas, small intestine, large intestine, ovaries, uterus, bones, muscles, lymph, skin. They were all positioned almost identically to a human. The only real difference was the existence of the organ that excreted the nerve toxin for her claws.

Apart from reduced organ function, everything else seemed okay. He couldn't find any clogged blood vessels, risk of aneurysm or cancer, or anything that could be a direct cause of death. No viral or bacterial diseases either. Her impending death was clearly the result of old age.

In that case, the approach to take was simple, but not easy. First, he had to select from one of three choices.

The first choice was for Vandal to use death attribute magic to prevent the breakdown of her cells while another life attribute mage activated her organs and restored their failing functionality. This method had been used on Origin, but it wasn't possible here because they didn't have a life attribute mage on hand. With access to nothing but death attribute magic, Vandal could only accelerate the death of her cells. He was unable to provide them any additional strength, like someone with life attribute magic could.

If this were just a physical injury, then I could hold her mortality at bay while applying a potion, but a potion can't stop aging.

The second method was to take measures to extend her life—to stop her from proceeding further toward death. This was a simple and effective method. If Vandal applied his techniques on a semi-regular basis, Zadilis would be able to continue in her current state.

But I can't do that either. To put it another way, all that could do was maintain her current situation. If he was treating massive blood loss or an allergic shock, pushing back her death would allow natural healing to take effect, but when it came to old age, all he would be doing was buying some time. There would be no healing, meaning Zadilis would remain frail and weak. It would also require regular treatments from Vandal, meaning his departure from the grotto would be a death sentence.

That didn't work for him either, then. It would let him learn her techniques, but it felt like he would just be keeping her alive to leech from her and then let her die.

Which left the final method: the most difficult, and the one that the researchers on Origin had never achieved. That dream of humanity—"Rejuvenation."

The restoration of youth. The process of removing "age" from cells and making them young again. Their experiments had successfully reduced the ages of the skin, bones, and other certain body parts, but none of their experiments had ever successfully rejuvenated all of the cells in a body. But during those experiments, Vandal's mind and body had been controlled by someone else. Since dying on Origin and being reborn in Ramda, he might have had fewer magical skills, but he had far more raw magical power.

Time to muscle my way through again. First, he allowed his Spirit Body arms to flow through every part of Zadilis. He tried to respect her moans while expanding his Spirit Body to fill her capillaries, skin cells, and right to the end of her nerves.

"Rejuvenation," he said. With that, he started to remove the "death" from her body, making her groan again.

A skilled fire magic user didn't directly control fire, but heat. That allowed them to not only apply heat and turn steel to liquid, but also sap heat away and turn the ocean into ice. That was why Vandal could, in theory, use his death attribute magic to control death, freely killing or taking death away, leaving life.

"Urk—urgh!" Zadilis gasped.

He gradually removed the aging—the death—from within Zadilis, like whittling down an accumulated mass. It was slow, but Zadilis did start to get younger. Her cells started to strengthen, and her organs started to recover.

"This is really burning some MP!"

The technique was sucking away magical power like nothing he had used before. Giving Zadilis back just one year cost him close to ten million MP.

"Boy, what—what are you doing . . . unnngh!" But she didn't seem as pained as before. In fact, now she was enjoying it. He needed to take his time and slowly rejuvenate her entire body, and so it was much better—much easier—for him that she wasn't suffering.

"I'm making you young again," Vandal replied.

"Making me young?! Is such a thing even . . . possible—" Then she broke off into moaning again.

"To be more accurate," Vandal continued, "I'm simply removing the old age from your body. So you aren't going to turn back into a little kid or anything like that." He wasn't turning back time, so even if he rejuvenated her beyond her actual age, she wouldn't turn back into a fetus or vanish completely. He was removing the death, which conversely was almost like moving her closer to it. If he did the same thing with a human woman, she would probably stop reverse-aging in her mid-teens. If he experimented and tried different techniques, maybe he could find a different way to turn a human back into a fertilized egg.

"Aaaaaaaaah!" Zadilis cried.

There was a thread of pain combined with pleasure, like a full-body massage, filling her arms and legs and body and even her head. It felt like a skilled masseuse was pushing her toward a happy ending, and she couldn't keep her mouth closed through the sheer pleasure. It felt like she had expelled all the air in her lungs as the pleasure also melted completely away. She panted for a moment or two before speaking.

"Boy?"

After catching her breath, she looked at Vandal to see him fallen over on his side. His arms had been removed from her body and were back to their normal physical form.

". . . I've burned all my MP. It's been a while since I pulled that off. I need a nap," Vandal managed.

It had taken everything he had to restore about ten years of life to Zadilis. He had barely been able to end the Spirit Bodification of his arms, and then he collapsed and fell asleep.

"It wouldn't have hurt you to explain things a little more clearly," Zadilis gasped, but her eyelids also looked heavy. The lethargy she had been feeling the last few days was gone, and yet her body felt as exhausted as if she had just completed intense exercise. But she also felt like she had energy to spare. It was a strange feeling.

The feeling of exhaustion came from the changes to her body happening in such a short period of time. It had been easier on her because ghouls stopped physically aging at the time of their first pregnancy. If Zadilis had been human, she would have passed out by now.

"Well, whatever. He's done something for me, and it seems like something good. I think I'll get some sleep too." She drew the already slumbering Vandal over to herself and fell asleep right there.

The young ghoul Warrior Banado had noticed their elder and their guest—who was now practically a member of the grotto—go missing partway through the festivities and had gone looking for them. Now he was standing in front of Zadilis's house, swallowing hard at what he had witnessed.

He had seen the two of them go into the house together. Then he had heard Zadilis's moans coming through the walls.

"Vandal and elder? Getting it on? Dhampir crazy, doing it so young!" Banado's lion-face twisted into a leering grin. He realized he was going to have to stop treating the baby like a baby. He was already a man—no, a king.

The next day, Vandal explained exactly what he had done to the newly energized Zadilis. She was both impressed by this application of death attribute magic and scolded him for not sharing the details before going ahead.

"Still," she continued, "it doesn't change the fact that you've saved my life twice. My most heartfelt thanks. If you were a Tamer, boy, I'd be willing to let you tame me. That's the gratitude I have for you. I'll have to think of something else, of course."

Among Vida's new races, those races with monster roots could be tamed. Due to their human-level intellect and divine roots, the chance of it succeeding was very low—unless the individual in question consented to the taming. Zadilis had brought the topic up not only because she wanted to repay the debt she felt at having been rejuvenated, but also because of the appeal she felt at the idea of going along with Vandal. Her heart longed for that, even as she knew she couldn't easily cast aside her position.

"I'd be happy to have you along, Zadilis, but the grotto needs you too," Vandal said, bringing her back to reality.

"Yes, that's true. They can operate fine without me, but I'm worried that they don't have a Mage to replace me yet," she admitted. She had thought they would be fine without her, not so long ago, but getting some years back made all the difference. She wanted to teach the young ones even more than she wanted to teach Vandal, and she also wanted to see her youngest, Basdia, have her first child.

"I haven't mastered non-attribute magic or magic control yet, anyway. I'll be around a little longer at least."

"Yes, true. Hearing that does put me at ease. Let us recommence the training at once!"

". . . My MP hasn't fully recovered yet. I need a little more time."

They ate a breakfast of gobgob and then got back to it. From that day forward, each training session ended with a rejuvenation session for Zadilis. The best way to grow one's MP was to use it all up. MP would increase upon leveling up, but also worked like other stats and skills, increasing with frequent use. But Vandal had too much MP to make use of this method up until now. Vandal had more than one hundred million MP. If there was magic that used 10,000 MP, he still needed to cast it 10,000 times to use his MP up. If each time took him only ten seconds, that would still be 100,000 seconds. That would be approximately 1666 minutes, or twenty-seven hours. Longer than a whole day. But when using Rejuvenation on Zadilis, it didn't even take ten minutes for him to burn through all of his power and pass out.

His schedule therefore settled into non-attribute magic and magic control training in the morning, making walnut sauce and gathering acorns around noon, followed by a baby nap, more training in the evening, and then using Rejuvenation on Zadilis on her and passing out at night. He would sleep through the night from there, and then repeat it the next day.

It was a pretty tough schedule, but that was somewhat alleviated by his creation of millstone golems. He could order them to "spin" and then drop in some roughly broken-up, boiled, dried acorns, and golems would automatically grind them for him. This solution was more eco-friendly than electric millstones on Earth, that was for sure.

Of course, Vandal and Zadilis kept the use of Rejuvenation a secret. It wasn't that they didn't trust the ghouls of the grotto, and ghouls lived for so long anyway that most of them wouldn't be that bothered about becoming young again. The same went for other monsters too. After all, most monsters were going to die in combat long before they reached the end of their natural lifespans. It was pretty rare for any of them to live as long as Zadilis had. The concern was if anyone who knew about Rejuvenation got captured by adventurers and spilled the beans. That would be bad. A massive bounty would be placed on Vandal, and a horde of adventurers and mercenaries would come sweeping in to capture him. Once capturing him, they would strip his freedom from him in any number of humiliating ways, and he would spend the rest of his life extending the lives of nobles and kings.

Vandal didn't want that as his future, nor would any in the Ghoul Grotto, which would surely be destroyed in the process. So they had decided to keep it secret.

"How is your magical power coming along?" Zadilis asked.

"Not even one percent per day. I guess a molehill will eventually make a mountain. Perseverance pays off. Something like that," Vandal said.

"One percent, for you, is over one million," Zadilis replied wryly. "That sounds way too big for a molehill."

With each passing day, Zadilis grew younger. She was a ghoul, meaning her appearance didn't undergo any major changes. But she was more dynamic, her voice was firmer, and there was a sparkle in her eyes that few could miss. Her appetite returned too, and her hair and skin seemed to recover their luster. The other ghouls started to take notice.

The only thing that was clear was that every night, Zadilis and Vandal went alone into her house, and didn't come out until morning. If you listened closely, you could hear Zadilis's muffled moans. And with each passing day, Zadilis was getting more energetic and alive.

Of course, this quickly led to misunderstandings. A one-year-old baby could never do such a thing, but Vandal was a different race from the ghouls. Maybe there were differences they didn't know about. Maybe a dhampir had that ability. He did act like an adult, far beyond his physical appearance. It didn't take long for the ghouls to start jumping to conclusions. The rumor mill started churning.

"Is the dhampir what's amazing here, or is it Vandal?"

"Maybe I'll ask him to give me a turn?"

"And maybe I shouldn't have said 'if I had a daughter' and instead gone for it myself!"

"That crusty old elder is acting like a young girl. If that isn't love, what is it?"

"I shouldn't be one to say—but he be good next chief!"

"Vigaro! You definitely should be the one to say that! You're the chief!"

"I propositioned him when he first got here, but he said he couldn't do it."

I wonder if we should let the young master know all of this talk. But if the rumors are true, it would be rude to bring it up.

Maybe we could just come out with it? Ask if it's true, dad?

Wow. I know he wants to become a noble in the future. Maybe we have a chance too? Sam and Saria's concerns were blown aside by jokes from Rita.

After his second birthday, as summer came on in full in July, Vandal finally acquired the Level 1 Non-Attribute Magic and Magic Control skills. He was happy to have achieved in less than a year what he had been told could take numerous years, but Dalshia and Sam were quick to point out that Level 1 was hardly anything to boast about. The magician among the adventurers who attacked Zadilis had Level 2 Non-Attribute Magic, for example.

"Still got a long way to go," Vandal murmured, but he was in a good mood. He felt proud. There was a chance that non-attribute magic didn't exist on Origin, meaning Vandal might now have a leg up on Hiroto Amemiya and the others still living their second lives there. A small leg up, maybe, but continuing to take such steps would help him protect himself in the future.

The MP training of exhausting his magical power by using Rejuvenation on Zadilis also came to an end. The reason was simple—Zadilis had reached the same age as her physical appearance.

"We don't know what will happen if you carry on. That's more than enough, anyway," Zadilis said.

"Yup. You should have more than 200 years before you start worrying about old age again," Vandal said. It had really provided a boost to his magical power, meaning he would have liked to continue, but there were no other ghouls in the grotto over 250 years old. If they used Rejuvenation on too many of them, then they wouldn't be able to keep the technique a secret, so they decided to stop. If he had another chance to fight some bandits, maybe he would use Rejuvenation on them first before finishing them off.

Vandal was pondering these things while cracking acorns with his nails, removing the inside, and preparing them for boiling. Then he noticed the ghoul female who was helping him. Not that he didn't know she existed—the grotto was large for a gathering of monsters but small for a settlement, and Vandal had already learned the names and faces of everyone living there. He definitely hadn't reached the level of best friends with all of them, but he could greet and chat with them casually.

"Bildy, can I have a moment?" The ghoul was called Bildy. She had been one of the excitable ghouls he had met at the banquet on the day he arrived in the grotto.

"What is it? Should I be breaking them up more?" She had a puzzled look on her face, but it was her belly Vandal was looking at. During the banquet she had definitely mentioned being pregnant. That was October last year. Now it was July, meaning around nine months had passed. He didn't know how far along she had been back in October, but she surely should be showing more now.

"No, I was just remembering—you said, if your baby was a boy, you'd name it after me," Vandal ventured, wondering partway through if he should really be asking such a question so casually, and so his voice started to trail off.

"Oh, you remembered that?" Bildy didn't sound offended, at least. "I'm sorry. I was pregnant, but I didn't carry the baby to term. If I have another, let me use your name then."

"I see. Okay, next time—huh?"

The casual nature of the comment, yellow eyes narrowed, tongue poking out, threw Vandal off for a moment. He had to make sure he had heard her correctly, but it seemed that he had.

"That was such a shame. No one had a single child last year."

"I lost mine before even two months. You lasted the longest, didn't you, Bildy?"

"I think so. I was almost at three months." The other girls were being casual about it too, and didn't appear to be putting a brave face on things. They did seem to think losing their pregnancies was a shame, but in a very nonchalant way, and as if it were completely normal.

"Oh! Once you're done with Elder Zadilis, maybe I'm next?"

"Hold on, Van! I should be first—"

"Basdia, there's something I want to discuss," Vandal said, seeking to derail the strange direction the conversation was headed. "Can we have a moment?" Vandal asked Basdia. He picked her because he was closest to her behind only Zadilis and Vigaro.

He heard other comments from behind—"I'm next after Basdia," from Bildy, and then "Why can't I be next?" and "No, it's my turn!" from the others. If he had been physically capable of performing such acts, he would have been happy to hear the comments, but he wasn't, and so he ignored them.

"Van, I'm happy you chose me, but it's still a bit early in the day—"

"Basdia." She definitely had the wrong end of the stick, and he quickly cut her off. "I'd like you to help me understand your attitude toward losing those babies."

"Why don't they sound sad about it? I mean, Van. It's because few babies ever make it to term," Basdia explained.

Ghouls had issues as a race with getting pregnant in the first place, and then suffering from early miscarriages once they did. There was no hard data to be found on actual pregnant rates, or the ratio of children successfully born. But it had long been said that maybe one in five babies made it to term.

It was the perfect recipe for a society with few children, but the 300-year lifespan of ghouls probably offset that issue. At least, it had until now.

"I think they aren't that sad . . . because this is just normal. There are some ghouls who cry for days when they lose their child, but they are rare. You probably think it's strange because that kind of behavior is more common for humans," Basdia reasoned.

It was just normal, so they weren't sad about it. They were just accustomed to this happening. On Earth people wouldn't believe such a casual reaction to the loss of a child, but this was a different world and a different race. A totally different situation.

After all, they had been living like this for hundreds of thousands of years. It was obvious from the grotto that they had little contact with other races. That meant they didn't think what they considered to be normal was anything out of the ordinary. If the ghouls had lived with other races, they might have started to wonder why they couldn't seem to have children so easily and felt more grief. But for the ghouls it was simply a case of "it's always been this way, so what can we do."

This was also linked to the timing of the majority of the miscarriages. They happened early in the pregnancy, before it really showed in the belly, and before the women started lactating. There were no sonograms in this world anyway, but even if there were, the fetus wouldn't even have an identifiable gender at that point. That all meant there was little feeling of having lost a child.

"Still. I don't think it's a problem to be discussed so cheerfully. Just my take on it," Vandal said.

"Yeah, I guessed as much." Basdia seemed to have noticed this difference between ghouls and humans for the first time from Vandal's questions. "We've only had goblins, kobolts, and orcs to compare ourselves with until now—and then we've only really been annoyed at how quickly they procreate as proof of how much weaker than us they are."

That gave Vandal a thought—maybe this jealousy had been the fuel for the ghouls working out such inventive ways to eat the other races.

"Thanks for sharing, anyway," Vandal said. "That makes a lot more sense now. It's been on my mind for a while. Especially not seeing many kids around here."

In fact, he had never seen a child in the grotto. Never heard a baby crying. Once or twice he had thought he was seeing a child, for a moment, but it was just a ghoul female whose first pregnancy had come when she was still very young, like Zadilis. It had struck him as strange that this was a settlement of more than one hundred adult ghouls, and yet there were no children. At first, he had wondered if maybe they were keeping the young ones away from him and his friends, as a precaution. Then he got caught up in the magical training and such concerns faded away.

The truth, however, had simply been that there were no children here. If Vandal had shown more of an interest in the topic, Zadilis or Vigaro would have probably just told him right off the bat. It wasn't an important secret or anything like that.

It also explained why the ghouls were such sexual creatures. It was hard for them to get pregnant, and then they lost four out of five of those pregnancies. That definitely applied some pressure.

"I suppose then there's nothing we can do about it." Vandal was willing to leave the issue there. It was a problem the ghoul race had faced for hundreds of thousands of years, and yet they had survived. They weren't sitting around straining their brains to resolve the "issue," because they didn't even see it as being one. The grotto itself was proof that their race wasn't in direct danger. They weren't asking for his help, so he didn't need to start sticking his nose in.

Of course, it would be a different matter if they asked for his help.

Basdia paused. "Maybe there's nothing we can do, but we haven't had any children here for more than ten years now. My mother and Vigaro are starting to get really worried. Mother's magic can't do anything about it, but maybe your magic could, Van? I want to get pregnant myself too, and when that happens, I want to give birth."

With that, she asked for his help. Now it was a different matter.

"Okay. I'll give it some thought."

Name: Vandal
Race: Dhampir (Dark Elf)
Age: 2 years 1 month
Alias: None
Job: None
Level: 100
Job History: None
——Status

Vitality: 42
Magical Power: 113550000
Strength: 37
Agility: 13
Muscle: 39
Intellect: 60
——Passive Skills

[Brute Strength: Level 1] [Rapid Healing: Level 2] [Death Attribute Magic: Level 3]

[Resist Maladies: Level 3] [Resist Magic: Level 1] [Night Vision]

[Spirit Pollution: Level 10] [Death Attribute Allure: Level 3 (UP!)]

[Skip Incantation: Level 1] [Enhance Brethren: Level 1 (NEW!)]

——Active Skills

[Suck Blood: Level 3] [Limit Break: Level 2] [Golem Creation: Level 2]

[Non-Attribute Magic: Level 1 (NEW!)] [Magic Control: Level 1 (NEW!)]

——Curses

[Unable to carry over experience from previous lives] [Unable to enter existing jobs] [Unable to personally acquire experience]

"Alongside my training, I'm going to start taking a look at this issue with your lack of children," Vandal reported to Zadilis.

Her eyes immediately opened wide.

"That makes me . . . very happy to hear, but you aren't talking about kidnapping women from other races and using the ritual to turn them into ghouls, right?"

"That's really a thing, is it?"

Dalshia had suggested it was, from the information about ghouls going around in the human world, but Vandal had assumed it was just a scaremongering superstition.

"Yes, it's possible. We've never done it here at this grotto. The only women we could really try it with here in this demon barren would be adventurers, and the risk of that is pretty high. Even if we pulled it off, it would attract all sorts of adventurers coming to wipe us out. Increasing our women would be the least of our problems."

The procedure wasn't as efficient as, say, the one used by vampires, due to conditions such as only working on women, but the ghouls did indeed have a way to transform other races. Using that to compensate for their low birth rates must have been another tactic used by the ghouls in the past. But the grotto had no access to women from other races other than adventurers, and they didn't want to take that risk.

"That said, it's true we haven't had any children here for ten years. We can't very well survive just by having you rejuvenate everyone in order, either. It would be great if there was a solution. We can all help out. You've mastered Rejuvenation, something even masters of life attribute could never pull off, so maybe you can do this too." It almost seemed reasonable for Zadilis to think this way, based on the impossible stuff the baby who just turned two had already done.

"I'll give it the best shot I can," Vandal replied.

From his perspective, there was no proof he could pull it off. His biological knowledge came from TV and school on Earth, and what he had absorbed from the dead researchers on Origin. And all his knowledge came from access to devices such as ultrasound and microscopes in the case of Earth, and things like life attribute magic on Origin. He wasn't a gynecologist! His confidence in reaching a solution was definitely on the low side.

And yet Vandal's death attribute magic had made a contribution to medicine on Origin that even Rodocolte had been forced to admit. Maybe he could solve this infertility problem.

"I'd better keep it a secret from mom," he said. Dalshia wouldn't want her two-year-old son getting involved in this field. *So this is how children get secrets from their parents*, Vandal pondered.

The method he selected was for ten healthy ghoul couples to "perform" for him. He used Spirit Bodification and Detect Life on them before, after, and even during the act, confirming their reproductive organs, semen, eggs, and other organs were all in working order. The causes that he discovered were simple but fundamental.

Firstly, the semen of the male ghoul could only survive inside the female body for around half a day. That was a lot shorter than when compared to humans. Furthermore, the egg of the female ghoul only lasted for six hours after ovulation. That was also incredibly short when compared to humans. The ovulation cycle was the same as for humans, however, only coming once a month.

"In most cases, either the sperm or egg, or both, are dead before anything can happen. That's why you can perform every day and still get no results," Vandal said. The ghouls had no means to measure the ovulation cycle, making the timing an especially difficult hurdle for them to overcome.

"Okay, that does make sense. But one thing—why do you keep calling it 'performing,' Vandal?"

". . . I'm at an age where I'm too embarrassed to spell it out," he eventually replied, managing not to look at Bildy. The girl was lying on a firm wooden bed, just having "performed" herself. *On Earth, the subjects would normally be the ones having difficulty with research or treatment like this.* It was a strange feeling. He was happy to be getting results, and keen to pursue answers. But it still felt strange—disconcerting? Depressing? He wondered why he was feeling that way.

Probably because he was researching the infertility of a bunch of cute girls. He had finished his lives on Earth and Origin without any experience with the opposite sex, and now he was going through this on Ramda. It didn't seem fair. It was all Rodocolte's fault, of course. *Yes. Blame it on Rodocolte.*

"So what can you do to stop this sperm and egg and whatever from dying? Can you stop that?" Bildy asked, breaking off Vandal's expressionless thinking. She didn't seem to know exactly what she was asking about, but her question was right on the money.

"I can," he replied.

Extending the life of the sperm and the egg would be easy for him. With Vandal's death attribute magic, he could keep a human suffering a clearly fatal wound alive for days to come. Keeping a tiny sperm or egg alive for longer wouldn't be any issue at all.

"Really? We've solved it already! Yay!" Bildy leapt up from the bed and swung Vandal around happily. Vandal couldn't join in her celebrations, however. He could do that much, but it still wasn't the fundamental solution he might have desired. In order to achieve such a solution, he needed to proceed further.

"Okay. Next, I want to look into preventing the miscarriages," Vandal said.

"But we don't have any pregnant women at the moment," Bildy said. Then she gave a sparkling smile, which made Vandal feel strange all over again. "Of course! We just need to get pregnant!"

After using death attribute magic to extend the life of the sperm and egg, it didn't take long for Bildy and the others to get pregnant. Vandal sensed the vitality of the receiving egg and became certain that the issue there had been the sperm and egg ceasing to function so quickly. It also didn't take him long to work out why so many female ghouls lost their babies early in the pregnancy: the fertilized egg lacked vitality.

He used Spirit Bodification to confirm that there were no external factors at play, such as sickness, and that the issue didn't lie with the mothers. But no, it was just an innate weakness in the eggs. Furthermore, the hardy vitality of the mother's cells saw the egg and fetus in the womb as invading presences and started to attack them. That was why so many pregnancies failed so early.

Once he knew the causes, this was also an easy fix. He could use death attribute magic to keep the egg and fetus alive. He just needed to extend the fetus's life and wait for the fetus to gain strength.

In December, with the ghouls' cold breath clouding the air, they finally saw results.

"Bildy and the others are so happy that they have your assurance. Of course, everyone else is too," Basdia said.

"Indeed. We'll be welcoming new lives to our grotto, boy, thanks to you. You have my deepest thanks," Zadilis added.

They were gathered with Vandal in one of the sunken homes.

"Now we know that three months of life-extending measures stabilize the pregnancy, so long as the girls are careful," Vandal said.

Three months into the pregnancies, the fetuses started to display amazing vitality, completely blowing away the prior weakness. He had kept an eye on the women for the rest of their pregnancies, but there was nothing to suggest daily attention was required. The issues with ghoul babies boiled down to whether they could get pregnant in the first place, and then make it through the first three months.

"Interesting. It's long been said that ghouls cannot have children outside the demon barrens, but it sounds like that might be possible after all," Zadilis commented. Monsters were energized when inside the demon barrens, allowing them to reproduce and their children to grow up more quickly than when living outside. It truly was survival of the fittest, and that was why no matter how many monsters adventurers killed, the demon barrens could always cough up more.

The ghouls were half-monster, so the demon barrens influenced them too. Even under that influence, they struggled with a lack of children. So leaving descendants behind outside the demon barrens seemed impossible. There might be plentiful monsters to feed them inside the barrens, but there were also plentiful monsters more powerful than them—and yet the ghouls had been left with no choice but to live there.

"Now I just need to make some magic items that contain the magic to extend the lives of the egg and sperm, and to delay the death of the fetus," Vandal said.

"Right. We can't keep asking you to do all of this yourself," Zadilis agreed. They knew the causes of the ghouls' problems now, and how to fix them. But at the moment, that would mean Vandal applying magic to the ghouls every single day. Vandal still planned on heading to the Olbaum Electorate Kingdom, and his time to do that was limited. Furthermore . . . working under those conditions wasn't good for his sanity.

"You aren't bad at learning magic, boy, but you don't excel at things like alchemy," Zadilis commented.

She wasn't wrong. Vandal was trying his best, but it wasn't going especially well.

There were two types of "techniques" on Ramda. One was anima magic. The other was techniques such as alchemy and anima magic.

Attribute magic simply came down to one's own synergy with each attribute. Zadilis had an affinity for light and wind attributes, for example, while Vandal had death attribute at his command. Techniques like alchemy and anima magic, meanwhile, were skills that applied one's affinity for certain attributes in various ways.

For example, anima magic allowed one to communicate with anima of the attribute one had an affinity for. A user provided MP to these anima spirits and they would perform a variety of magical tasks in exchange.

Alchemy, meanwhile, involved skills that applied magical power and magic to various media to create potions or magical items.

There were no death attribute anima, so Vandal had no access to anima magic. But if he were to learn some alchemy, he would be able to create death attribute magical items. This possibility had already been proven on Origin, where scientists siphoned off his magical power to create a litany of items. Of course, Vandal's freedom had been stripped away from him on that world, and so he had no idea how to use such techniques. The knowledge he had obtained from the souls of the researchers was rooted firmly in the high-level technology used to create magical items that existed on Origin, so it was useless in his new life.

He was therefore learning alchemy from scratch from Zadilis, but it was giving him more trouble than non-attribute magic and magic control.

"It might really be next year before I can set off again," Vandal commented. "What about you, Basdia? While I'm still here, you can have a baby if you like?" Basdia hadn't participated in Vandal's research like Bildy and the others, and so still wasn't pregnant. She had seemed very keen on the idea, but when Vandal asked, she just told him she didn't want to try yet.

"If I get pregnant now, I won't be able to serve as a test subject once you make your magic items after learning alchemy," she replied.

"That's true, but aren't you worried about your age?"

Ghoul women stopped aging at the point they first got pregnant. Basdia hadn't gotten pregnant yet, and so her appearance was twenty-five . . . no, twenty-six years old. She was blisteringly hot and looked very young, so Vandal didn't think she had anything to worry about on that score yet.

"Are you sure?" Zadilis asked. "The results seemed confirmed already, and the boy thinks maybe you should. We won't be so lacking for test subjects, so you don't need to worry about that."

"It's fine, mother. Van said he doesn't care about my appearance, even if I get a little older," Basdia replied.

"That makes it sound like you've settled on Van to father your child."

"You'll be waiting more than ten years for me," Vandal chimed in. "Please go ahead and get pregnant before that."

Rumors of Vandal and Zadilis having such a relationship had done the rounds through the grotto at one point, but that misunderstanding had since been corrected.

But Basdia still shook her head in reply. "Sorry, I didn't make myself clear. I'm not planning on having this baby with Van. But I am looking to curry some favor by being a test subject."

"Curry favor for—what?" Vandal asked, a little puzzled. He had left transactional society behind since coming to live here—if he had ever really been a part of it, at least in this lifetime—and so this took him a little by surprise.

"To have you father my second child, Van," Basdia said.

"Um... Like I said, that's a tough hurdle for a two-year-old."

"Don't worry. I'll wait until you can perform."

"Hmmm. That sounds like an agreeable relationship to me, boy," Zadilis said.

"No. It's not," Vandal retorted. Basdia would stop aging with her first pregnancy, leaving her young and beautiful for the remaining nearly 300 years of her life. That would mean she could stay the same for the ten-plus years it was still going to take for Vandal to reach adolescence. But even if he could "perform" biologically, he wasn't going to want to start fathering kids as soon as it was possible. "I won't be able to take on the responsibilities of a father at such a young age. I'm not human, either. I'm a dhampir born from a vampire and a dark elf. We don't even know if I'll be able to have kids with a ghoul."

"Nothing to worry about on that score," Zadilis informed him. "All of the new races created by Vida should be capable of interbreeding."

"Great. That's good news, right, Van?"

"Yeah. That wipes out my best refute." Sometimes he didn't need a 300-year-old around dropping knowledge.

"You're a male, Van," Basdia said. "You don't need to worry about fatherly responsibilities or whatever else you were talking about."

"That's right. Men should concern themselves with risking their lives to secure food. Raising children is women's work," Zadilis agreed.

"Maybe that's how ghouls see it," Vandal replied. The men weren't exactly getting off lightly in ghoul society, to say there was the "risking their lives" part in there.

"But we are ghouls," Zadilis said simply.

"True. But we don't know if the baby will be a ghoul, or something else. A human father seems to produce ghoul babies, but I'm a dhampir."

"Hmmm. You've got a point there," Basdia conceded, but she didn't look ready to concede. "I won't hold you to 'as soon as biologically possible,' then. Just whenever you're ready, Van.

I bet you're going to live much longer than humans too. I might have had a change of heart myself by then."

The last part was clearly just to try and throw Vandal off the scent, but he also couldn't fire back with "you'll never change your mind!" So he was left with just an uncomfortable sigh.

"If I do have a change of heart, you can perform with my daughter," she added.

"Give me a moment to catch my breath!" Vandal exclaimed. "This is a lot of pressure to put on a two-year-old!"

"Hmmm. That would mean my great-grandkids would be fathered by you, boy. That's not a bad proposition either," Zadilis cackled. "If I have any more daughters in the future, you can service them too!"

"What are you talking about, mother? Think of your age! You are over 290! You already said I was a difficult birth!" Basdia exclaimed.

"Huh? That's true, but I've been feeling somewhat rejuvenated of late. I can probably pop out a few more yet," Zadilis replied, dropping all sorts of bombs without a care in the world.

"Where is this coming from, all of a sudden?! Your age and resulting lack of magic almost got you captured by adventurers two years ago!"

Basdia, who still thought her mother's natural lifespan was coming to an end, flew into a bit of a panic. She had no idea that Vandal had rejuvenated her back down to the age she actually looked, so her confusion was understandable, and unlikely to abate anytime soon.

Vandal chewed on an acorn cookie from the sidelines. Basdia had been running rings around him a moment ago, and now her mother was doing it to her. Like daughter, like mother. It was a sight to behold.

Then he swallowed the cookie, and realized they still had a lot of work to do.

Vandal acquired the Spirit Body skill!

An arrow whistled past her ear.

"Kachia, that Goblin Archer is aiming for you!"

"Sort it out, Rikken!"

"Easy for you to saaaay!"

The five adventurers were locked in combat with some goblins and an assortment of other monsters. The female adventurer Kachia barely avoided the incoming arrow from the Goblin Archer. Rikken pulled back his bow and unleashed his own arrow, but it was stopped by a hobgoblin that was protecting the Kobolt Mage.

Their enemies included kobolts and hobgoblins. Such a mix was always a possibility in dungeons, but races never worked together in a regular demon barren. Hobgoblins were one thing, as they could live alongside goblins at times, but it was bizarre to have kobolts in the mix. Monsters simply never worked together. The concept of cooperation didn't apply to them. Even if different groups of monsters encountered a party of adventurers at the same time, they wouldn't think of cooperating to take them down. They were enemies forever—enemies, and food.

There were a few exceptions to this rule. One was monsters being controlled by humans. Legendary Tamers were said to have been able to command vast hordes of monsters at the same time, but there was no reason for such a legendary Tamer to have unleashed this group of monsters. So in this case, a different exception was at play.

"Don't tell me we're dealing with a monster king!"

Kachia unleashed a blinding-fast Circular Slice with her bastard sword, chopping a Goblin Soldier clean in two.

"A king?" her shield-bearing ally shouted as he used his trusty shield to beat down a Kobolt Rogue. "Don't joke about that!"

But even Rikken had to admit it was a possibility. Monsters of different races could also work together when they were being controlled by a more powerful monster—a powerful individual with the intellect and desire to rule monsters other than themselves.

Sometimes, very rarely, such a monster with the appellation "king" was known to appear among demi-humans. To clarify the threat such monsters posed, adventurers' guilds designated these kings as natural disasters. If a king had appeared, and now goblins and kobolts were fighting together, that likely meant . . .

"Bugooooh!"

As though providing evidence to these terrible suppositions, a pig-like roar—albeit a powerful-sounding pig—rang out, and then a cluster of large shapes emerged from deeper in the forest.

Orcs. And these were Orc Knights, outfitted with armor and shields. And behind them, looking down over the fighting—

"Damn! A third wave!"

The shield-bearer triggered Stone Wall and Stone Shield battle techs in quick succession, staking the honor of his shield on desperately trying to allow his allies to escape, but it was like one man trying to hold back an avalanche.

A normal orc was around two meters in height, but Bugogan's massive frame was over three meters. He reclined on his chair, made from a plant-based monster called an Ent, while listening to the reports from his aids and sons.

"Buhgy, bumohgy, fugooh, buhmo."

Weapon and armor production was going well. Every orc and slave had been given gear suited to their skills, and there were reserve stores as required. But one of the kobolts who made their gear had gotten worn out.

"Buhmo! Buhmomon! Buhgy!"

Training of the soldiers was also proceeding smoothly. At a single word from Bugogan, they would crush any enemies without any fear of death. That went without saying, these being inferior races, but he preferred pawns that he could use. Their loyalty was essential.

"Buhgogon, bugy'gy, bugebubohoho! Buhhohoho!"

They needed some more slaves. Goblins and kobolts multiplied like bugs, but they had lost significant numbers in an attack on that ghoul grotto, so they weren't back to full strength yet. He gave orders to supplement their numbers—but outside of the territory of that particular ghoul settlement.

"Bugogogo, bumoh, fubo-wo-bugyagyah!"

They also still needed females. The useless inferior hordes should be satisfied with goblin and kobolt females. That was what wild orcs had done until now. But there were also higher-quality females around, and after seeing them, it was hard for the trash not to desire them.

"Bugoh . . ." He gave a sigh. The child of a weakling would be a weakling, whether it was carried by a goblin or a better class of female. Bugogan wondered why their tiny brains couldn't see it. But he was the leader of these weaklings now, and it was true that he needed even more minions to lead.

"Bugoh, ghoul fugogo, bumomo!"

If they continued to attack the grottos, that other settlement might notice what was going on, but no matter. He ordered his orcs to attack more grottos and capture female ghouls. Those orders made all the orcs leer and grin, not just the one who had complained about the lack of females. Even the Orc Mages, known for being far more intelligent than normal orcs, were unable to contain their desires. *This is the problem with orcs*, Bugogan thought to himself. These inferior races were so weak, so foolish—so *inferior*. But that was why they had to be ruled by one such as him. The orc among orcs. A Noble Orc.

He stroked his golden, mushroom-like hair, deciding he could forgive the foolishness of his minions.

Sometimes a king would appear among goblins, kobolts, or orcs—a rare and powerful leader. But they remained a king purely within their own race. The higher forms of these were superior to all lower races. Such races included the High Goblin, High Kobolt, and Noble Orc. They were far stronger and lived far longer than the lower races. Noble Orcs had received that title a little ironically, due to sharing their appearance with the fat and nasty human nobles, but that irony didn't diminish the fact that a Noble Orc was always at least rank 6. Considering normal orcs were rank 3, a noble one was clearly far stronger. They were intelligent and lived as long as humans. They could use magic and had the strength to command lower races unconditionally. Even a gilded Orc King would kneel before the most average Noble Orc.

Bugogan had come not from this small, jungle-like demon barren, but a massive demon barren that covered the mountains on the south of the Vangaia Continent. A Noble Orc empire reigned there. However, he fled after defeat in a power struggle. After surviving the trek through the mountains, the defeated orc had discovered a burning passion to command and control upon arriving in the jungle. All his passion and hard work were focused on bringing the lower races under his control, building his own empire, and then eventually taking over the human nations too.

He had brought the varied orc settlements in the demon barrens all under his control, wiped out the lower-functioning orcs that peppered them, and elevated those with any shred of actual intelligence. They captured goblins and kobolt females, and Bugogan had even made children using the ugly, filthy goblin females himself to increase the number of pawns he could use. At the same time, he kept his presence secret from the ghouls and adventurers, biding his time.

Ten long years of that allowed Bugogan's empire to achieve substantial strength. Continually weeding out the weaklings left him with three sons, 300 orcs who survived training, and around one hundred goblin and kobolt slaves each. They also had a few dozen domesticated magical beasts.

If the adventurers' guild knew of such a large gathering of monsters, they would quickly designate them a disaster and bring in a horde of rank B adventurers from across the country. Bugogan therefore worked to hide himself from adventurers. His minions knew to only attack when they could be sure to kill or capture the entire adventurer party.

The other race Bugogan had avoided too much interaction with was ghouls. A single ghoul was on an equal footing to an orc in terms of strength, but they were also smart. Goblins and kobolts would happily fight even among themselves, but ghouls would put aside their differences and fight together against a common enemy. Bugogan wasn't afraid of losing to them, but he also wanted to avoid losing too many of his minions. So when attacking ghouls, he had always picked small-scale settlements and been sure to wipe them out entirely.

From among such target settlements, the most troubling was one of about one hundred ghouls, led by that old Ghoul Mage. They had numbers, and every ghoul was also immensely powerful. Prior to Bugogan's arrival, orcs had been nothing to the ghouls of this settlement other than slightly strong but easily taunted and highly delicious meat. He hadn't wanted to mess with the settlement led by that particular Ghoul Mage. But now one of the kobolts Bugogan had taken as a slave had some good news for him.

That Ghoul Mage was soon to die of old age.

"Buhmomomo, fugo, fugoho." Bugogan gave the order and the only non-orc monster in the throne room stepped forward.

It was an aged kobolt with graying fur. This aged kobolt was something rare even in the large demon barrens Bugogan originated from—a Kobolt Shaman. It had protected its place in Bugogan's empire by using its ability to talk to spirits and provide useful advice to Bugogan as a result. The fact the Ghoul Mage would soon die from old age was a prophecy brought to him by this Kobolt Shaman.

Now, however, the Kobolt Shaman's ears were lying flat, and its shoulders shaking. It was muttering to itself in a muffled voice but didn't seem to be communicating with a spirit. An Orc Mage listened to those mutterings and then reported what the Kobolt Shaman was saying to Bugogan.

"The Ghoul Mage should have died of old age by now, but for some reason she's still alive. She's unlikely to die unless we can kill her. I don't know why, but the spirits there won't obey me recently, so I can't find out what is happening," the mage relayed.

After hearing all of this, Bugogan stroked his hair for a moment or two, thinking quietly—and then took up his beloved demon blade from the side of the throne and swung it down at the Kobolt Shaman.

A squeal and a splatter.

After ordering the remains—split from head to somewhere around the waist—to be taken away and used for rations, he wiped the blood from his blade. He had only kept the pathetic creature around because it had seemed useful. That report suggested otherwise. It had been completely wrong about the ghoul! These dogs strutting around on two legs really were just a waste of space.

"Bugogo! Bubobio, bukonbuon, buhho, buhihibumo!"

Bugogan had been thinking the day would end with nothing but bad news, but there was a good report too. His oldest son, Bubobio, had led some slaves and minions to capture a party of adventurers, and they had been successful. One of the five had been killed, but the remaining one male and three females were injured but alive. The news of capturing the adventurers stirred up his minions. In particular, the news of three females among them.

"Bugobu, buhhihibu, buhoho, hibuhibuhi."

First, though, they needed to extract what information they could about the human society he sought to eventually conquer. Human females often didn't last a night of attempts at mating.

"Buhoho."

In this case, the females would become mothers and the male food. His son Bubobio had particularly proven himself, and would be rewarded with one of the females to be exclusively his.

Rewarding good service was an important part of being a ruler.

A week passed.

The winter air was comparatively clear, for the humid jungle, and Vandal took another breath as he powdered up herbs, minerals, and magic stones to create media for alchemy. Then he suddenly froze.

"Boy, if you can't concentrate harder than that, it really will take you years to learn these skills . . . boy?" Zadilis started to caution him on his hands stopping, but then noticed something was wrong.

He was staring into the empty air, tilting his head and shaking it, and making general noises as though he was holding some kind of conversation.

"Boy. Are you pushing yourself too hard? Maybe we should end our training for today." Zadilis spoke a little hesitantly, worried about overexerting him, but he looked at her and shook his head. So he hadn't started hallucinating from exhaustion. That was something.

"The spirit of a Kobolt Shaman just told me that there's a

The Death Mage

49

large orc settlement deep in this demon barren, presided over by a Noble Orc who considers this grotto to be a threat."

Bugogan's secrecy was therefore defeated by a leak from a spirit.

"As it turns out, I'm going to be risking my life in another battle. Same as always, so nothing to worry about," Vandal said.

Vandal. Those are hardly words that would put a parent at ease, coming from their child.

"You want to stop me?" Vandal asked.

Hmmm, no. You're right. It isn't the first time, and I know you'll do your best to stay alive. Make sure you work together with everyone else, Dalshia said to him.

"I will, mom," he replied.

It took seven days for the spirit of the Kobolt Shaman, having been split in two by the demon sword, to travel to the grotto and warn them of the settlement created by the Noble Orc. It also gave other useful information about the attacks on other ghoul settlements and the capturing of adventurers. Vandal had been a little uneasy at first about whether the ghouls would believe it, but Zadilis and the others did so without question. It made him happy to feel trusted.

"300 orcs, one hundred goblins and kobolts. What should we do? Can we win?" Basdia wondered.

"So there 300 enemies?" Vigaro asked.

"500, you fool. You can't even count?"

"Goblin, kobolt, even orc, no enemy for us! One of us kill five of them, we win!" Vigaro replied.

"Hey," Bildy said, "you aren't including all of us in those numbers, are you? I'm pretty pregnant at the moment."

"It's Bildy's fourth month of pregnancy. She can't fight," Zadilis said.

"Not to mention, they are led by a Noble Orc," Basdia said. "Even the weakest Noble Orc ever would still be stronger than my mom or you, Vigaro."

"What! You think I lose?!" Vigaro shouted.

"Yes, you lose! We'll definitely lose!" Basdia shouted back.

"No, no lose! Vigaro no lose!" He was insistent, if a little cowed.

"Face reality, you big lump!" Basdia countered.

While Vandal thought the problem over himself, the ghouls were also having a serious discussion about how to handle the issue of this orc settlement. It was a matter of life and death, after all.

The ghouls were seated in a circle around the firepit in the center of the grotto, holding an emergency meeting to determine the response of their settlement. Vandal was also taking part.

"Boy. Tell us the enemy numbers again," Zadilis asked.

The gathering was tense, so she asked him to repeat the information from the Kobolt Shaman. After relaying its information to Vandal, the kobolt's spirit body had quickly broken down. Even after death, it had used its experience as a medium to converse with other spirits, and then taken a week to arrive at the grotto, seeking revenge on the Noble Orc who had killed it. Maybe that revenge was the only thing that had driven it. Perhaps Vandal's Death Attribute Allure skill also played some part, even from so far away. There was no way to know, but after providing that vital information, its remains lingered dozily around Vandal now.

"There are 300 orcs, one hundred goblins, one hundred kobolts, and then some beast-type monsters. Overall, we're looking at close to 600 enemies. They are led by a Noble Orc who has three sons. There are also decent numbers of Orc Generals, Orc Knights, and Orc Mages, while the goblins and kobolts include some Soldiers, Chiefs, Knights, and Mages. But there are no other generals or kings. The enemy has already attacked a number of other grottos and taken ghoul women to birth their children. They have also recently started attacking parties of adventurers."

This report of the strength of the enemy, the lengths they were going to, and the attacks on other ghouls—different settlements, but same race—brought further consternation to the faces of the gathered ghouls.

There were only male orcs, both normal and noble. That was why they were forced to take women from other races in order to procreate. They often used female goblins or kobolts, or even female cattle that they stole from villages. But because they were monsters created by the demon king and his brethren to specifically bring harm to humans, they preferred human women above all else.

Ghouls were treated as monsters in human society, but their women looked exactly like humans apart from small things like skin and eye color. As their roots lay with the goddess Vida, from the perspective of monsters, they could be considered human. The ghoul women had such difficulty getting pregnant, and lost so many of their pregnancies (without Vandal's help). But for some reason, things went a lot smoother when partnered with orcs. Not that anyone present was happy about it.

Maybe orc reproduction looks like standard fare, but is actually some special form of parthenogenesis? Vandal pondered, applying some of his scientific knowledge from Origin. *If orcs reproduce not using the egg of the female, but by orc DNA absorbing DNA from the mother, it could also explain why the children always take the father's primary characteristics. I have no idea if DNA exists in this world, of course. It doesn't sound like this could help to solve the infertility issue, either.* Vandal was going off on a bit of a tangent, while the ghouls had taken his information and were discussing again what to do about it.

Opinions seemed to be broadly divided into four camps.

The first was simply to wait out whatever the orcs were doing. "They are targeting human villages and towns. That's nothing to do with us. We can just keep out of it." The ghouls espousing this solution suggested it was too dangerous to risk a conflict, even if ghouls had already been taken and more grottos were going to be attacked. Zadilis and the others had no responsibility to protect the ghouls from other settlements, that much was true. It sounded cold, but trying to help out would be pointless if it only got them eradicated as well.

This was also the wrong move. The Noble Orc who led them had been waiting for Zadilis to die. The only reason he might have been waiting, logically speaking, was to attack the grotto once she was gone. Such hordes of monsters were generally a dictatorship, with their one leader deciding everything. In this case, that leader had set his sights on them, so they were unlikely to be able to stay on the sidelines.

Humans might sign treaties of non-interference or take other such political measures, but monsters didn't think like that. Even if the Noble Orc did leave this grotto alone, there was the future to think of. If the orc's attack failed, this demon barren would be inundated with adventurers. They would hunt down the remaining orcs and seek to ensure that such a force never rose again. The Milg Shield Kingdom was at war with the Olbaum Electorate Kingdom. They had a powerful army and many adventurers. That meant the Noble Orc was going to fail eventually, almost certainly.

"How about we run for it while the orcs are rampaging?" another ghoul offered, but then soon changed her mind. "No, that wouldn't work."

Escape for one hundred ghouls was simply not a practical option. The jungle demon barren wasn't small, but it would still be hard for one hundred ghouls—including pregnant women—to hide themselves from a bunch of orcs. They might have considered running to a different demon barren, or even trying to live outside them, but the ghouls had lived here for so long that they knew nothing about the geography elsewhere. Dalshia and Sam had a little more of that knowledge, but they could still only say that it would take more than ten days to reach another demon barren after leaving this one. And if they tried to escape the demon barren, it was highly likely humans would happen across them.

As for the mountain range, no one knew the land over there. Vandal had made some bug and small bird undead and sent them off that day, just to cover all their bases, but it would be at least a month before they could provide any intel.

"You're not going to suggest we surrender to them?" Bildy said. "No way! If that's the only option, I'd rather die."

Indeed, choosing to give up and join the orcs was completely out of the question. The males would be used as slaves in combat, no better than goblins or kobolts, eventually to be crushed in battle against humans, while the females would be used for breeding. It was no better solution than fighting and losing.

"We have to fight. We can contact the other grottos."

In the end, Basdia's suggestion was the only real option. They needed to fill in the gaps in their numbers as much as possible and then attack before they were attacked. *Things are going to get busy again*, Vandal thought.

"Then I must say something first," Vigaro, the next chief, said. His tone was grave and he looked directly at Vandal. "Vandal, you leave grotto at once."

"No thanks. Moving on, I have a proposal—" Vandal said, immediately turning down the suggestion.

"Stop, stop, stop! No change subject!" Vigaro wasn't ready to let it slide so easily. "You fight orcs with us! You okay?"

"Yes, I'm fine with that. Back to my proposal—"

"Not fine! You listen me—"

"I'm not leaving," Vandal said abruptly.

"No interrupt!"

Vandal had already done that a few times, he had to admit. Maybe his word choice was the problem. He had been a bit off-hand, but then he hadn't wanted to come across as bossy either. If word choice was the issue, he wasn't sure how to correct it. Vandal tilted his head, still thinking it was a communication issue, while Vigaro's facial hair bristled with anger.

"This fight between ghoul and orc! Not you! Not your fight!"

Vandal had been in the grotto for a while now, but he wasn't a ghoul. He had talked of his plans to leave and head over the mountains to the Olbaum Electorate Kingdom. Sharing his fate with the ghouls was not the right thing, surely. He was a two-year-old child. He shouldn't be getting dragged into a fight with such an uncertain outcome.

"It is my fight. I'm your friend, your ally, and your family. Now can you please listen to my proposal?"

But that two-year-old was also in command of the conversation. He had to blurt out his feelings, keeping his tone as neutral as possible, and tried to change the topic again.

"What you even do?!" Vigaro shouted, although he barely managed to keep a smile off his face from being called "family."

In truth, if everyone in this world were to be sorted into the strong and the weak, Vandal would still fall on the weak side. He did have a massive pool of MP, and his dhampir physiology allowed him to exceed a grown man's strength even at two years of age. He could also use death attribute magic, something almost no one in this world was even aware of.

But putting it another way, that was all he had. He had no training with martial arts or weapons, and his knowledge of warfare and tactics was all self-taught. He didn't have a special knack for strategy.

His massive MP pool was also just that—a massive pool of MP. He couldn't use it to kill anything directly. And if his Vitality dropped to zero, he would still die regardless of his MP.

The MP was fuel for magic, of course, but Vandal could only use death attribute magic and non-attribute magic. Death attribute magic was weak when it came to delivering direct attacks, and he was still barely getting a grip on the basics for non-attribute magic. He could use Magic Sucking Barrier to nullify mages, but this time they were fighting orcs. There would only be a small number of Mages. The orcs would be using brute strength and raw power as their primary weapons.

Ever since Dalshia's death, Vandal had been painfully aware of all this. But at the same time, he was aware that he did have options.

"First of all, if you keep me around, I come packaged with three Rotten Beasts, one Phantom Bird, a Skeleton Soldier, and Sam, Saria, and Rita," Vandal pitched.

That gave Vigaro a start. Sam and the others were all Vandal's minions. If Vandal was going to fight the orcs, they would all fight too. They were all rank 3 or higher, providing a considerable boost in combat strength.

"Furthermore, I think I'll be useful when contacting other grottos," Vandal continued. They already knew that his Death Attribute Allure skill worked on ghouls, and that could be a big help in this situation. It was another good point, and so Vigaro could only accept defeat.

"That's enough, Vigaro. We all know you're only thinking of the boy," Zadilis said.

"More than enough! Van is our family. He's one of us!" Basdia said.

"Enough, enough! Vigaro, just let him fight!"

"I know you're lying, but you still shouldn't say this has nothing to do with him!"

It was turning into a real pile-on. Vigaro didn't look ready to die on this hill either.

"All you! Ah! I care not! You prove you part of this, and I never say not you fight again!" he grumbled.

"The next chief has given his approval, boy. Can we hear your proposal now?" Zadilis said.

Vandal sighed, finally getting the go-ahead to reveal his plan.

"It's nothing much. I just thought you might be able to use the armor and magic items I have no other use for."

From the expressions on their faces, it certainly didn't seem like they thought it was "nothing much."

Like so many other things, magic items in this world were ranked. From the bottom up, the ranks were Inferior (sometimes called "Initial" to avoid negative connotations), Medium, High, Special, Legendary, and Divine.

Inferior grade items were pretty simplistic for having the name "magic" items. They made everyday life easier in small ways, including swords less prone to rust, armor you could sleep in without getting stiff, timers that would ring in one hour, magical hotplates, and magical lanterns.

They started to become more conventionally magical in the Medium grade, the level of item that adventurers start to carry. From High grade, the retail price jumped up, and the difficulty to obtain them too, and Special grade items were often treated as genuine national treasures. Legendary grade applied to things like holy swords that only chosen heroes could equip, while Divine applied to the kind of artifacts and cheat items that appeared in only the myths of old.

These rankings weren't only decided purely by function, or the strength of the magic the item carried, but also the difficulty of creating the item, the materials used, and their rarity. Before magical hotplates became easier to make, they had been ranked as Medium, for example.

"Come on, everyone. Line up."

The dungeon-made magic items Vandal was giving out to the ghouls were classified from Inferior to Medium. When he first obtained them, he had known nothing other than the fact they were magic items, and the amount of magical power they contained. Even after learning the non-attribute spell Appraisal, the results of its use were still based in Vandal's own knowledge, meaning he still didn't know what any of them were.

Now, though, for the sake of this difficult task of taking down the orc settlement, he was handing them out—free of charge, of course—in order to enhance the fighting strength of the ghouls. It was generous of him, perhaps, but he hadn't been using them for anything and he had no way to convert them into cash. He hadn't worked hard for them either, as he had either gotten them from the dungeon undead or just found them in chests. He wasn't attached enough to worry about giving them away.

"This one is a low-grade agility and strength enhancer. This one, a low-grade stamina recovery accessory. Both offer little more than a placebo effect, but they are definitely magical items," Zadilis reported.

"Then they go to Gudan and Gibly," Vandal announced.

Zadilis was appraising the items, and Vandal was giving them out. If he had sold these in a large human town, they might have fetched 1,000 Amidd. Not a cheap price, but not unobtainable either. Here in the demon barrens, however, they were precious items that everyone was more than happy to receive.

It's a whole new feeling, making people happy by giving presents. Vandal hadn't had any real friends on Earth—or even a real family—and on Origin he had been a test subject. Ramda had finally given him a chance to give presents to other people, and Vandal felt very happy about that.

"I crush all orcs!"

"I repay this armband with orc meat buffet!"

Apparently, orc meat differed from goblins and kobolts in that it tasted delicious even without any special preparation. It was said to be like wild boar, and Vandal was looking forward to trying it.

"Vigaro can have this powerful battle-axe that the Skeleton General gave me. The kite shield can go to Basdia," Vandal said. Putting aside the armor and weapons used by Saria and Rita, he was now giving out the best of the magic items they had obtained in the dungeon.

Vigaro offered a "thank you" for the battle-axe, and then continued with a serious look on his face.

"Vandal. You become king."

Vandal did a double take. "Excuse me?"

"When ghoul face powerful enemy, band strength together. One at top king. You that."

"Me?" Now Vandal did a triple take. Vigaro had effectively explained what a king did, but Vandal wasn't sure why he was being offered such an important role. He was asking for confirmation, but Basdia seemed to take it as affirmation.

"You'll do it? Thank you, Van!"

"Hold on, hold on! I wasn't agreeing. I was just making sure you really want me to do it!"

"Everyone thinks you're the one!" Basdia said.

"Everyone? Like who?" Vandal fired back.

"Everyone other than you, Van."

"When did that happen?!"

The decision had seemingly been made while he was giving out the magic items.

Congratulations, young master.
You're going up in the world!
We need to do better too!

Sam and his daughters were listening in. There didn't seem to be a single dissenting voice in the house. Sam's pale white spirit body was giving a thumbs-up—or a "Sam's-up," one might say—while Rita and Saria were clapping happily.

Ah, Vandal. Just look at you! Dalshia smiled as she watched the scene, happy tears on her cheeks. Maybe she felt like the mother of a child becoming class president, or head of the student council.

"Wait, wait, wait. Let's just hold on a moment here. You might all accept this, but what about the ghouls from other settlements? I'm a dhampir. A different race. Why should I be king?" Vandal said, not willing to give in so easily.

"No worries. It'll be fine," said Zadilis.

"Absolutely fine. They would have a problem if you were human, but as a dhampir? No worries," Basdia added.

"I suppose I can see that," Vandal admitted. The ancestor of the ghouls was thought to be the sibling of the ancestor of the vampires. That made a half-vampire like a dhampir something like a relative to ghouls. In the Amidd Empire and its nations, dhampirs were also designated as monsters. To top things off, Vandal had the Death Attribute Allure skill. He was pretty sure the other ghoul settlements wouldn't have too big a problem with him taking the role.

"In terms of both abilities and practicalities, you are qualified to act as our king, boy," Zadilis said. She knew that Vandal had picked up the Enhance Brethren skill, because he had discussed it with her when he noticed it the other day. "You told me about the Enhance Brethren skill, didn't you? As you would expect from the name, that skill enhances the stats of your brethren—which in your case means undead, and us ghouls. If you become king and lead us, the ghouls who follow you will therefore all get a boost. That skill is more or less exclusively for use by a king."

Enhance Brethren was a skill that every monster with "king" in the name had. It was the skill that made the hordes led by a king stronger than normal monsters, and bolstered their numbers. Zadilis didn't know this, but it was said that a goblin with Enhance Brethren level 10 had led a horde of goblins capable of fighting fully armed knights while armed with just wooden sticks and hide armor. There were reasons why the adventurers' guild designated the appearance of a king as a natural disaster.

Zadilis continued, "You are also helping to resolve our fertility issues. You see a brighter, more prosperous future for ghouls, and have made good progress toward that already. It feels like you're suited to lead us."

It seemed like a bit of an exaggeration to Vandal, but the difficulties with having children were an issue faced by all ghouls, and being unable to easily expand their numbers was a definite shackle upon them becoming stronger. The other settlements were likely to happily sign up to follow Vandal once they learned he held a solution to this problem. Vandal placed a hand on his forehead, a little dazed that his work with the fertility problem would lead to all this. Vigaro, meanwhile, was looking quite pleased with himself. Vandal was now very much a part of all this, but he still wasn't sure how to feel about it.

"Very well. I will become king."

And so, long before he could become an adventurer, Vandal became a Ghoul King.

Vandal obtained the title of Ghoul King!
Enhance Brethren level increased!

His first job as king was fitting armor.

"Gudan, is it too tight? Anywhere your movement is too restricted?" Vandal asked.

"Hard to move elbow and neck. Helmet tight," the ghoul reported.

Male ghouls had a lion-like face and arms so long their knuckles basically dragged on the ground. They were quite different from humans, and so they couldn't use Vandal's armor collection without some modifications. Adjusting the armor to fit the ghouls would normally have taken a skilled craftsman and a considerable amount of time.

"Rise!" Vandal commanded.

He had come up with a method that didn't require either of those things. First, he had the ghoul put on some armor, and then he went ahead and turned it into Living Armor—or, to be more precise, golems.

"The shape of the armor is going to change. Try moving your arms and neck," Vandal said.

Metal squealed as he used the Golem Creation skill to change the shape of the armor. It wasn't perfect, but it allowed ghouls to use the same metal armor that humans wore. It was rough, with no fancy decorations, but functionally it worked. The long arms created a shortage of certain parts, but he could add leather sections from monster armor to cover those up.

"Wow! Feel good now!" the ghoul exclaimed. "Thank you, king!"

"No problem. Next!" Vandal said.

This didn't feel like an especially royal task, but armor makers in the Ghoul Grotto only worked with monster hides, bones, and horns, so they couldn't adjust metal. Vandal had to do this for them.

There was more regal work on the horizon, anyway. Tomorrow they would start visiting other ghoul settlements to seek out their aid. The settlements were laid out so that their hunting grounds didn't overlap, and so they weren't especially close. Without a shared enemy, they were rivals at best, and so Zadilis actually didn't know their exact location or numbers.

The plan there was to use the undead bugs released by Vandal and information from spirits to locate each destination. It might have all seemed a little laid back, but they had time. The Noble Orc wouldn't make a move until spring, at the earliest, if not summer. Of course, they wanted to rescue the captive ghouls as quickly as possible, but if they rushed into things and failed as a result, then no one would be rescued at all.

The ghouls were less interested in saving the captured female adventurers. After all, under normal circumstances these were two opposing sides. Basdia and Bildy did seem to feel bad for them, as women, but they weren't willing to risk their lives for them.

Vandal had no interest in saving them, either. In his case, adventurers from the Milg Shield Kingdom were also his enemy. Even if they did save them, Vandal could easily see them turning around and trying to start claiming some bounties from their saviors.

I'd probably feel differently if I'd seen the conditions they are being kept in, or if it was someone I knew waiting to be saved, he thought. Vandal was aware of his own trauma on this topic. If he saw a woman in peril, or being hurt, it reminded him of Dalshia and pushed him over the edge. *We'll just do what we have to, as quickly as we can, and if they are alive after we've won, we can save them then.*

If he just let the captive adventurers die, he had no idea what the cheaters who would be reborn here in the future might say about it, and so, ultimately, he planned to save them.

I wonder if I should explain to the Zadilis and the others the exact position I'm in here? he wondered. *Hmmm. Maybe once we resolve this current crisis. Zadilis, Vigaro, Basdia . . . I could tell those three. If they're dragging me into their stuff, I may as well drag them into mine.*

Vandal was thinking about whether that would even the score when the next ghoul to be fitted stepped up. It was Basdia.

"Basdia? Anywhere that's too tight for you?" Vandal asked.

He was still having a little trouble adjusting to having become her king. The female ghouls were much more human-shaped, unlike the males, and so he hadn't expected to need to adjust the armor much for them.

"It's a little tight . . . well, a lot, around the chest," Basdia admitted.

". . . Right. This is mainly male armor." Vandal realized that almost all the armor was going to need refitting, in one way or another.

Golem Creation, Limit Break, Resist Maladies levels increased!

Name: Vandal
Race: Dhampir (Dark Elf)
Age: Two years six months
Alias: [Ghoul King]
Job: None
Level: 100
Job History: None
——Status
Vitality: 47
Magical Power: 113551200
Strength: 40
Agility: 16
Muscle: 42
Intellect: 75
——Passive Skills
[Brute Strength: Level 1] [Rapid Healing: Level 2] [Death Attribute Magic: Level 3]

[Resist Maladies: Level 4 (UP!)] [Resist Magic: Level 1] [Night Vision] [Spirit Pollution: Level 10]

[Death Attribute Allure: Level 3] [Skip Incantation: Level 1] [Enhance Brethren: Level 2 (UP!)]
——Active Skills
[Suck Blood: Level 3] [Limit Break: Level 3 (UP!)] [Golem Creation: Level 3 (UP!)]

[Non-Attribute Magic: Level 1] [Magic Control: Level 1] [Spirit Body: Level 1 (NEW!)]

————Curses

[Unable to carry over experience from previous lives]

[Unable to enter existing jobs] [Unable to personally acquire experience]

The Death Mage

Chapter Two

STRATEGY FOR A KING

The Noble Orc's band was planning on attacking humans, but there were concerns that they might attack the Ghoul Grotto first. The ghouls had become like Vandal's own family, and so he took on the title of Ghoul King and decided to fight alongside them.

In that moment, Vandal was caught up in his alchemy training. He was using a mortar to crush up ingredients as he applied a fixed volume of magical power. He was working with kobolt bones, kobolt magic stones, dried organs from a Poison Toad, and his own blood. He then used this mixture to draw a magic circle, and if that functioned as a magic item, then he had been successful. If it didn't, then he had failed. Whichever the result, he was to repeat this process until he learned a new skill. The content of the mortar might change, but the content of the training remained pretty much the same.

They were facing a powerful foe—500 monsters, including goblins and kobolts, led by a superior Noble Orc. With such a threat on the horizon, and after taking the title of Ghoul King, Vandal had to wonder if this was really the best use of his time. Even as he sat here grinding with this mortar, the captive females were being subjected to all sorts of orc horrors!

But Vandal wasn't thinking about any of that stuff as he continued to grind the ingredients.

"Panicking and rushing into things will only make them worse," he muttered. That was his policy, and the policy of the ghouls too. He was gathering information, of course. He had released more undead bugs, sending them to search for the Noble Orc's settlement and the locations of other ghouls, and the ghouls had dispatched envoys to the other grottos they remembered. There was no need to rush into things until that information came in. The orcs wouldn't make a move until spring at least, while it was currently December, right before midwinter.

Orc pregnancies lasted for six months, and then it took six months for children to reach adulthood—the same kind of fever-pitch breeding as goblins. While they were waiting now, Vandal didn't plan on giving them too long to build their numbers.

"I'm really not getting this skill," he muttered. It had been a number of months since he started learning alchemy, and he hadn't learned a single skill yet.

"That's how these things go," Zadilis replied. "You are faster than most monsters, trust me. Maybe not so much compared to humans."

In principle, skills ranged from level 1 to 10. Level 1 was when someone was just starting out. For a combat skill, it might now be possible to use it in a real fight; for a crafting skill, it would be more of a hobby than a profession.

Level 2 was for a standard soldier, or a craftsman finding their feet. Level 3 would get some credit among adventurers or mercenaries for combat. For crafters, it signaled a certain quality, but still not enough to strike out alone.

Level 4 meant one was skilled in that area of fighting, a veteran. For crafters, it was the point at which working alone was permitted.

Level 5 meant a skilled combatant, averaging at grade C for adventurers. Level 6 was good enough to train nobles, and reach grade B as an adventurer. A crafter could have a shop in a large city at that level. Level 7 would attract attention at a national or noble level, and on anything less than a grade B adventurer, it would suggest some serious personal issues. A level 7 crafter would receive a stream of people looking for training. Level 8 made an individual famous across the land.

The names of those with level 9 skills would go down in history. Grade A adventurers came in around here. Level 10, meanwhile, extended into the superhero realm.

Very rarely, it was possible to exceed level 10, with the skills in question getting promoted to higher versions. Individuals who achieved such feats became objects of worship. They became known by such names as "Sword King" or "Fire Emperor," or simply as gods.

On Earth, the equivalent might have been someone like Musashi Miyamoto. That said, even he hadn't been able to fight an opponent for a week moving faster than the speed of sound, without any food or drink, or slice a rock harder than steel in two.

That was Vandal's appraisal of the skills in this world, anyway, based on what Dalshia and Zadilis had told him. Taken in that light, he could see why it took so long to acquire alchemy, and other skills like magic. However, there were other elements in this world that Earth and Origin didn't have: none other than job skill modifiers.

The people living on Ramda could acquire modifiers to their skills by taking jobs. These made it faster to acquire skills and level them up. In some cases, they allowed complete beginners to become skilled swordsmen or craftsmen in just a few short years—if, at least in the case of the swordsman, they didn't die prior to obtaining a sufficient volume of experience.

But to put that another way, it was difficult to acquire or level up skills in this world without taking a job. Even with a skilled teacher, the student would first need to be in a suitable job. From that perspective, Vandal was again an outlier, in that he was learning and leveling up his skills without any job at all. The curse he was under prevented his skills from reflecting his experiences from previous lives, but it couldn't make him forget the feeling of having once acquired that knowledge. That feeling aided him in learning such things again, and his massive pool of magical power allowed him to train ten if not hundreds of times more frequently than regular people. He also had the dhampir race modifiers.

As proof of all this, he had been completely unable to learn any combat skills, with which he had zero experience on Earth and Origin.

"This all means that it would be easier to learn this stuff if I had a job," Vandal mused.

"Yes. Pretty much," Zadilis agreed.

"You've given me another reason to hate this country."

Changing jobs required a special room only found in such facilities as a guild. In the Amidd Empire and its member nations, Vandal was treated as a monster, meaning he had no access to such amenities. Of course, even if he could access such a room, he had the "Unable to enter existing jobs" curse to deal with, meaning he was probably unable to change jobs anyway.

"But hatred isn't going to help me obtain these skills. Back to the grind."

"Yes. Well said, boy," Zadilis said, tousling his hair.

If she had known his Resist Maladies and Limit Break skills were also going up, she probably would have stopped his grinding on the spot. They were increasing due to dealing with the malady of overwork and pushing himself beyond the limits of his baby body. But Vandal had no plans to stop either. He had been pushing himself as hard as he could, ever since Dalshia got killed.

On the next day, they discovered the location of the other grottos. There were ten of them. But they only needed to take the time to visit four. The other six had already been attacked by the orcs.

The men . . . all the men, killed . . . and the women . . . ghooooul!

Gaaaah! My family, my clan, all burned! Burned by those pigs!

It hurts! It hurts! My mother was screaming! The pain! Ghooooul!

We attacked! Attacked those ghouls, under order from Lord Bugogan!
Ghoul poison doesn't work on us! Orc Mage magic protects us!

The spirits from the ghouls and the orcs killed during the fighting, which his undead bugs brought back to him, fed Vandal the information. Since time had passed since the attacks, some of the spirits were reduced to simply howling or repeating the same few words over and over, and even those that could manage better still spoke in fragments, but it was possible to piece together what happened.

Bugogan, the Noble Orc, had attacked the grottos in order,

starting from the smallest. Zadilis had the largest settlement by far, with the others being between thirty and fifty ghouls. The orcs attacked with a force of around eighty, including slaves such as goblins and kobolts, led by one of the Noble Orc's sons. Regular packs of ghouls often didn't have powerful individuals like Ghoul Mages or Ghoul Barbarians, with a rank 4 Ghoul Warrior functioning as chief in a more intermediary role in those cases. Such grottos could do little against the attack from a rank 6 Noble Orc. They also had numerous Orc Mages with spells that could provide resistance to the toxin from the ghouls' claws. That magic was applied prior to going into battle to all of the orc fighters and even some of the slaves.

The ghouls had still put up fierce resistance, and defeated many of the goblins and kobolts, at least—but the orcs were there to capture ghoul women, so losing slaves wasn't really a concern to the enemy.

In total, Bugogan killed more than one hundred ghoul males and took more than one hundred ghoul females as slaves. Ghoul females were far tougher and longer-lived than human women, making them excellent breeding stock. Everything pointed to Bugogan using the ghouls, alongside the goblin and kobolt females, to increase the numbers of his powerful orcs. The Kobolt Shaman likely hadn't known any of this because, in his role as a medium, he hadn't been a slave on the front lines.

"That means the orcs will increase by about one hundred per year," Vandal said. "Bugogan gives them something of a baptism by fire, just throwing them into live combat without prior training, which probably kills quite a few of them, but they're still increasing faster than ever. We need to rip their organs out of their living bodies and splatter their gray gook all over the ground."

"Boy, I know you are angry, but try to remain calm," Zadilis chided him.

"Yes. Cool head. Young always get so hot," Vigaro added.

"I'm not angry. The emotions from the spirits are just bleeding into me a little."

"That worse!" Vigaro exclaimed.

"Boy, the magical power leaking out of you at the moment looks like skulls. It is actually scaring me."

Both Zadilis and Vigaro were close to Vandal, but the sight of countless black skulls swirling around him was freaking them out. The ghouls from the other settlements meant nothing to Vandal, and he wasn't especially concerned. But after listening to all of the spirits for so long, he was unable to prevent a surge of anger at the orcs and their doings.

"There are only male orcs, which is partly the root of this problem," Vandal said. "This is what they have to do to keep their race going, and sexual desire is one of the three primary motivators, so it would be impossible to tell them to ignore it. Honestly, the ones at fault here are the demon king and the evil gods who created the orcs, who created monsters in the first place. But they're still really pissing me off."

"Vandal, you calm or not? Three motivators? What they?" Vigaro said.

"I don't know either," Zadilis said. "You seem to still be in possession of your faculties, anyway, which I am relieved to see. And there are still four grottos that haven't been attacked. We shall send envoys at once."

Talea gave her orders to the men of the grotto, and then settled back on her own handmade throne with a contented look on her face.

With her yellow eyes, brown skin, and nails purple with the toxins they secreted, Talea certainly looked like a ghoul woman. But as one could suspect from her human-sounding name, she was a ghoul who had started off as a different race entirely.

When she was human, Talea had been the daughter of a skilled craftsman. She proved herself from a young age to have inherited her father's skills, and it was hoped she would become even greater than her father once she came of age.

However, when a large trading company moved into their town, her parents lost their store. This forced them to make a difficult, and terrible, decision. They sold Talea into slavery.

Talea had talent, that was true, but she also had two younger brothers. At the time, whether a noble or peasant household, the family line always passed down through the male heir. Talea had greater skills than her brothers, was more technically proficient, but that only worked against her. She was sold, and her family got back their store.

Talea sold for a high price. She had her crafting skills, was very beautiful, and while young, already had the kind of body men loved to look at. Her buyer forced her to work as a prostitute, and this betrayal by her family caused festering wounds in her heart. After having to pleasure disgusting clients over and over again, she was unable to withstand it any longer. She decided to run.

When the moment came, she killed the client she was servicing and fled the brothel, then the town. In order to shake off pursuit, she entered these demon barrens. That had allowed her to escape her pursuers, but instead she had been captured by the ghouls.

She had thought they were going to eat her alive, and she gave up on life. But the pack that captured her was only small and didn't have enough females. They didn't want to eat her, but rather to breed with her.

After being forced through the ceremony, she was turned from a human into a ghoul. She lost all will to resist, and just gave herself over to the ghoul males, living her life listlessly under their instruction. Now that she was a ghoul, even if she ran away, humans would kill her if they found her. As she was originally human, she didn't know how to make use of her newfound ghoul strength or poison. Her only chance of survival was to go along with the males from the grotto, even if she could see little future in such a life.

She finally broke free from these days clouded with despair when the males returned from the hunt with the pelt of a Huge Boar. As Talea stroked the bristles, she recalled the past, and murmured that this would make fine armor. The males had heard her words and told her to make good on them.

She had obeyed, without question. Using the limited materials at her disposal, she had created leather armor for the ghouls that matched the quality of anything being sold in town.

From that moment, Talea became second only to the chief of the grotto.

She used the materials from the monsters hunted by the males to make all sorts of weapons and armor. She might have transformed from a human to a ghoul, but her talent for crafting remained intact. She used Giant Scorpion carapace to make shields, Iron Turtle shell to make armor, and Impaler Ox horn to make spears. The warriors from the grotto she belonged to started to hunt monsters with gear equivalent to that used by adventurers, obtaining the strength to fight off adventurers themselves.

As she regained her strength, she used the other skills she had developed as a prostitute to captivate the weak minds of the males, reducing them to putty in her hands. The other women became jealous of her, so she taught them the same tricks, bringing them onto her side—but also beneath her. One hundred years after becoming a ghoul, Talea stood at the top of the grotto while remaining the weakest one in the whole settlement.

In the one hundred years since then, a grotto that had been on the verge of collapse was now sixty ghouls strong, and ghouls from other settlements would come with food as payment to purchase Talea's wares. Their influence was beyond that of Zadilis's grotto, even though the mage had more than one hundred ghouls.

"Hehe. Maybe a decade more and I'll be ruling this entire demon barren," Talea cackled to herself. She sat on on her comfortable throne carved from an Ent, her body adorned with accessories created from gemstones taken from dead adventurers, and her luxurious black hair spilling out around her. With her mouth demurely hidden behind a fan skillfully created from whittled-down Iron Turtle shell, she really did look like a queen for all ghouls.

Of course, everything she wore she had made with her own two hands.

She had no contact with Zadilis and knew nothing of the orcs led by Bugogan. Her confidence in the realization of her ambitions was absolute.

"A humble human, fallen to a slave, becoming ruler of an entire demon barren of far more powerful monsters!" She chuckled. "The thought makes my heart sing."

"Lady Talea, make me shield!"

"Lady Talea, please make me some armor too!"

"Wait your turn!" she snapped at the ghouls. "You don't need to ask! I'll make whatever you need!"

Her daily duties as chief were coming to an end, she had thought, but then some ghouls interrupted her train of thought. Taking a moment to gloat over the future was part of her morning routine.

"Chief! We beat Metal Slime!" a ghoul suddenly announced. It was one of the warriors who had been out hunting last night.

"What?!" Talea stood up from her throne, her eyes sparkling.

The ghouls brought the Metal Slime fluid—transported in a leather gourd—and the silver Metal Slime core before her. The moment she saw them, Talea's face blushed and her body buckled, like a maiden reunited with a lost love.

"Oh my. Materials from Metal Slime, with both liquid and metallic properties! What weapon—no, what armor—should I turn these into? Ah, this is something! I need to think how best to use these!" She oozed lust even while discussing something completely unrelated to sex, but her ghouls were accustomed to such displays by now.

In fact, it made the other ghouls happy too. As chief, Talea made excellent weapons and armor, and from her time as a human, she treated those below her well. She was over 250 years old, at this point, so her perception as a woman was diminishing, but she was still a very popular leader. From Talea's perspective, she had grown into this ghoul stuff and now enjoyed a more fulfilling life than she had as a human.

"Chief! Message from scouts. Carriage coming!" said a young ghoul, arriving on the scene in a panic.

"Ah! Sounds like adventurers," Talea said. "How many of them?"

There weren't any monsters in the demon barrens who used carriages. It could only be adventurers. Her lovey-dovey reaction to the Metal Slime materials was gone in the blink of an eye. Her expression tightened up and her eyes became sharp and focused.

"The carriage surrounded by ghouls. Look like undead carriage."

"How many ghouls?" Talea asked. "If it is only a few, they could have been tamed by a Tamer."

The Tamer might have concealed themselves within the carriage, placing the tamed monsters on the outside, but there were apparently five ghouls with the carriage. Ghouls were a race with roots with the goddess Vida, but they were also mixed with monster blood, so they could be tamed. But it was far harder to do than for normal monsters. It would take a special kind of Tamer to have five ghouls and an undead carriage tamed all at the same time. Such a Tamer would not go to such lengths to conceal themselves.

"Ghouls from one of the other grottos might have picked up some rare undead," Talea reasoned. "Call out the remaining warriors. Protect me."

There were still half the warriors left in the grotto, so she didn't expect five ghouls and one undead to cause any strife, but she always erred on the side of caution. With her warriors guarding her, she headed out to greet the newcomers.

Just as reported, there were five ghouls around an odd-looking undead carriage.

"Stop right there. What do you want from my grotto?" Talea called out, surrounded by her horde of ghouls, and the carriage stopped.

"To talk. We have a common enemy. The other grottos who you have dealings with have already agreed to help," said one of the ghouls.

"A common enemy?"

When the ghouls faced a common threat, they would combine their strength and work together to defeat it. That didn't originate simply from being the same race—it also offered them the highest chance of survival. As a former human, Talea understood that approach, but being a former human, she was still suspicious. This might all be a plot to absorb her grotto for their own gains.

The ghouls were mumbling among themselves, reacting to the suggestion of a shared enemy. Talea silenced them by snapping her fan closed, and then looked at the ghoul who had spoken so far.

"Could you share some more details with me?" Talea asked. One thing Talea had learned since becoming a ghoul was that most of her kind had pretty simple personalities. They weren't cut out for deception or trickery. It was therefore best to keep questions direct and simple.

"Of course. Allow me to explain."

A small shape emerged from the wagon covering. The speaker was so small that for a moment, she thought she might have overlooked him completely in the shadow of the ghouls.

But no. She wouldn't have been able to do that. Such charisma radiated from the small shape that she almost bent the knee from simply being in his presence. He had long white hair, one bloody-crimson eye and one strange purple one, and skin so pale he looked sickly. He clearly wasn't a ghoul, and yet there was something about him, standing in front of her, that told her he was her superior.

Before she realized it, the other ghouls had indeed all dropped to their knees on the ground. Talea was unable to resist the urge to join them any longer, but just before she dropped to her own knees, the newcomer spoke to stop her.

"No need for that. You are Talea, correct? I am Vandal. I just recently became a Ghoul King."

This ball of charisma looked a little abashed at the ghouls worshipping him.

Monsters with "king" in their name, such as Goblin Kings or Kobolt Kings, could bring any others in their race whom they encountered under their control unconditionally. This effect was based on the primal instincts of monsters. The effects of the Enhance Brethren skill told them that by joining this new master, they could better not only themselves but their entire race.

That was what had started happening—in spades—when Vandal visited other grottos. He not only had the effects of Enhance Brethren but also his Death Attribute Allure skill, and the synergy between the two was quite something to behold.

"Amazing, King," said one of his ghoul guards.

"I didn't expect them to kneel just from talking to them," Vandal admitted. He was even impressing himself. It felt like he had become the prophesized hero in some tale of fantasy warfare. But having these adults, so much larger than him, all bowing and scraping before him didn't actually make him feel good. In fact, he felt apologetic.

He had lived for a total of close to forty years, across his three lives, but when considered objectively, his mental development had differed in each, running from seventeen to twenty-one and now two years and seven months. Vandal therefore lacked the sensibilities and awareness of an adult. He had simply been considering the skill effects that the title of Ghoul King would bring him, and he was shaken to see this side to becoming king.

They had heard about the Ghoul Queen Talea from the other grottos, and her influence over multiple groups of ghouls. When even she moved to prostrate herself before Vandal, he even felt guilty.

"That's why we would very much like to ask for the help of your grotto, Talea," Vandal finished explaining. "I'm not sure we can call it a 'reward,' but we should be able to make it worth your while."

He was being very polite, perhaps to compensate for everything else. Vandal had poor communication skills to start with, and so his basic approach to dealing with others was to try to avoid upsetting them. Under the current circumstances, he was taking that to new extremes.

"I see. And what kind of rewards are you offering?" Talea asked.

"Although we don't have them ready right away, I will be able to provide items that will resolve your general infertility issues, and also items to allow for more long-term preservation of food," Vandal said.

The ghouls had no currency, restricting the ways in which one might reward them. The only things Vandal could think of were the magical items for infertility, which he was planning to complete soon, and other magical items containing Maintain Freshness magic.

"Is that true?!" Talea exclaimed.

The suggestion of resolving the infertility issues made her and all the other ghouls immediately take notice. It was an issue faced not only by Zadilis's grotto, but the entire ghoul race. Vandal's suggestion that he could resolve it made them all look at him with wonder in their eyes.

The stress of all this is going to raise my Resist Maladies skill again, Vandal mused, but he didn't say anything. It would be selfish to ask them to be friendly, but then tell them not to get *too* friendly.

"In that case, we will happily join with you, Lord Vandal," Talea said.

Vandal flinched. "No need for the 'lord.' Just call me Vandal. Even 'boy' would be fine." He didn't feel much like a lord right then, in his two-year-old body.

"Oh my!" Talea exclaimed. Vandal wasn't sure why she was so happy. "In that case, Lord Van, it will be my pleasure to function as your aide."

He hadn't asked for it, but now Talea had become his aide. He couldn't understand what was happening.

Talea, however, in this moment, discovered a new ambition. The ambition to aid this young Ghoul King to expand his dominance beyond even these demon barrens, bringing glory to herself as his aide.

I never thought I'd get this chance, pushing 260! Talea thought. *Hehe! I was slammed down once but look how I've crawled back up to the light. And I'll keep crawling, until the moment I die!*

Her eyes were sparkling with fresh ambition. Unable to face them for too long, Vandal turned his own eyes aside to the spirit body of Sam, sitting in the wagon seat.

Young master. You are as popular with the older ladies as ever, Sam complimented him. It wasn't quite the kind of popularity Vandal was looking for.

Now that you have become royalty, you will find this kind of people flocking to you, Dalshia added. *This could be a good learning experience.* His mother had easily seen through Talea's intentions but seemed to think it could be a teachable moment. The only saving grace for Vandal was that the intense charisma Talea and the others felt from him would weaken once they joined him and received the effects of Enhance Brethren, fulfilling their basic instincts as monsters.

Enhance Brethren skill level increased!

Name: Talea
Rank: 3
Race: Ghoul
Level: 1
Job: Prostitute
Job Level: 100
Job History: Apprentice Armament Craftsman, Armament Craftsman - Slave (Forced Job Change at Level 47) Apprentice Prostitute
Age: 263
————Passive Skills
[Dim Vision] [Resist Pain: Level 1] [Brute Strength: Level 1]
[Paralytic Venom (Claws): Level 1] [Allure: Level 3]
————Active Skills
[Appraisal: Level 6] [Armor Craftsman: Level 6] [Weapons Craftsman: Level 6]
[Pillow Talk: Level 5] [Dance: Level 2] [Lovemaking: Level 2]

A strange woman continued alone through the demon barrens.

It was strange that she was alone, but not unheard of. The adventurers' guild recommended forming into parties, for the sake of the adventurers' own safety and completing quests efficiently, but solo activities were not prohibited.

But upon closer inspection, her gear and her mannerisms were not normal.

All of her gear looked brand-new and not especially fit for practicality. She wore the bare minimum in terms of unscratched leather armor, so small that it protected nothing beyond her chest and waist areas, and she carried a shield no larger than her own face. In her other hand, a simple steel sword.

Yet she proceeded through the demon barren without any signs of fear, taking down the low-rank Horned Rabbits and goblins that popped up along her path with a swing of the sword. She didn't collect the bounty parts or carve any materials from the monsters she defeated, seemingly uninterested in turning them into cash.

"Should be soon," she muttered to herself, with a voice that sounded lifeless.

That was when orcs suddenly appeared around the woman.

Not only was she completely surrounded, but at the back, there was a Noble Orc, standing more than twice as tall as a normal orc and with a mane of golden hair. The orcs were snorting excitedly as they told her to throw down her weapons. And rather than show any sign of resistance or hesitation, she dropped her short sword on the spot.

There was no fear on her face—or indeed, any emotion of any kind at all.

The female adventurer, having surrendered without resistance to the orcs, was tied up with thick vines and dragged away. The young Noble Orc holding her leash had a dirty grin on his piggy face, cackling as he handled her like some kind of pet. He was probably happy about how she would make a fine prize for his father, keeping him occupied and in good spirits for a while.

The female adventurer was dragged by the Noble Orc into the orc kingdom that her captor's father had created. It seemed as though her fate would be to breed monster children until her death, but there still wasn't a flicker of emotion on her face.

None of the orcs—even the noble one—noticed this oddity. Monsters weren't capable of reading the subtleties of the human face, and the Noble Orc didn't care about the expressions a woman might make anyway.

The long-faced man, who had been sitting back deep in his chair with his eyes closed as though sleeping, suddenly opened his eyelids and quickly pressed a handkerchief to his mouth. "How disgusting."

There was the stinking breath of the orcs, the laughter of the goblins, and the wily little kobolts. These pigs who thought they were nobles, presiding over a court of filth. And then the women, treated as nothing more than cattle, kept alive rather than being given the mercy of death.

The man had been prepared to see all of this and taken the job knowing what it would entail. Yet he still had trouble preventing himself from throwing up when finally presented with this sight.

"Are you all right, Lord Luchiriano?" the steward asked.

"I'm fine. Please, my good man, call the viscount," he replied. "I have something to report."

"Very well. I will go and fetch my master. My apologies, but please wait here for a moment."

The steward had only dropped in to see how things were

progressing, so he poured some fragrant tea and left. Presumably the idea was to drink that tea and recover his spirits prior to the lord arriving.

The wonderful fragrance of the tea did indeed help to make the terrible sights that were still burning in his brain fade away. But he had seen them for work, so he couldn't afford to forget them completely.

"Your reconnaissance has achieved results?!"

A handlebar mustache entered the room, loudly mouthing off about the secret missions. No, not a handlebar mustache—it was a noble sporting one. Luchiriano quickly put down his cup and gave the lord a bow.

"I have progress to report, Viscount Velnoh Valchez," Luchiriano said.

This noble, one Viscount Velnoh Valchez, was the lord of this region and the man who had hired Luchiriano. He was aged but kept himself trim and tidy, with few characteristics other than a fine handlebar mustache, but he wasn't inept. Just an average noble.

"My Living Dead has successfully infiltrated the orc settlement."

Living Dead. A special kind of undead, created using life attribute magic but still classified as undead. Magic was used to restore life to a fresh corpse with no pulse or respiratory activity. The resulting creature had a heartbeat and drew breath but didn't have a soul, meaning it was classified as undead. Visually, it was impossible to differentiate it from a living person. It was warm to the touch, and magic would detect it as being alive. It just appeared as a kind of expressionless person who talked in monotone.

The problem was that magic provided this life, meaning the corpse needed to eat and sleep. Unlike pure undead, it could also be affected by poison and succumb to disease.

Luchiriano had been hired by Viscount Valchez to use one of his Living Dead as a familiar, borrowing its five senses to confirm the truth of some unpleasant rumors. These were rumors originating from adventurers about a powerful nest of monsters that had taken root in a jungle-like demon barren that was further out from civilization.

For a while now, many parties of adventurers heading out to that particular demon barren had failed to return. At first, it had just been considered the whining of weaklings, but then a solo bandit had sighted something terrible. A Noble Orc, leading orcs, goblins, and kobolts.

Noble Orc was a higher race of orc, highly intelligent, that often formed hordes of monsters that could run into the hundreds. Luchiriano had been hired to see if the bandit had truly seen a Noble Orc, and if so, the size of the horde the Noble Orc had created.

"The Living Dead, under my control, was captured by a medium-sized group of orcs, led by a noble, and then taken to their settlement. The location is about three days' progress inside the demon barrens," Luchiriano reported.

"How many Noble Orcs are there?! What size is the horde?!" the viscount asked, mustache quivering.

"I confirmed the Noble Orc commanding the group that captured me, and the king of the settlement. That's two. But other clues suggest there is one or two more. In terms of the number of monsters, there are likely four or five hundred," Luchiriano continued.

"Three Noble Orcs, and 500 monsters?!" Viscount Valchez sounded ready to pass out at these numbers.

Noble Orcs were at least rank 6 monsters, with the most powerful among them potentially as strong as a dragon. There were at least two of those, and maybe four or more. If they were leading 500 monsters, the entire strength the viscount could muster—knights, town security, all the adventurers active in the region—wouldn't be enough to prevent a single word. Annihilation.

"However, the Noble Orcs—including the king—don't appear to be too powerful," Luchiriano said. "Of course, I mean purely relative to the potential of a Noble Orc. I think that grade B adventurers, leading around 200 grade C and D, would be able to handle the problem."

"Are you sure?" Viscount Valchez exclaimed, some blood returning to his paper-white complexion. But then he immediately gave a sigh. "This is still a crisis. We need to summon 200 adventurers and get some good ones too—grade B or higher. I'm not sure our knights and soldiers can handle combat with so many monsters." The viscount shook his head. "This situation is moving beyond me. I need to reach out to Marshal Palpapekk."

An indispensable skill for a leader was the ability to call on the aid of those above them when they couldn't handle something themselves. If he allowed his pride to make the decision for him, pushing him to handle the monsters alone, he risked not only failure but losing his entire domain to monsters. On this point, Viscount Valchez was a noble worthy of his handlebars.

"The Noble Orcs are planning to move in the summer," Luchiriano said. "There are still groups of monsters within the demon barrens who do not obey the orcs, and they are dealing with those first. Probably ghouls."

"Then at least we have a little time," the viscount murmured. "Good work, Luchiriano. I'll pay your fee to the adventurers' guild, but please keep the details of this request a secret. We cannot afford a panic among the people."

"Thank you, Viscount," Luchiriano replied, finally able to relax. At last, he made some bank. In the nations of the Amidd Empire, the Alda religion held powerful sway, putting all sorts of restrictions on the use of undead. He had been wanting to move on for a while now, and this was finally the money he needed to make that change. He would head to the neighboring Olbaum Electorate Kingdom and find a comfortable town that suited his talents.

"I will continue to submit designated quests for you, so please keep yourself available." Viscount Valchez's comment, however, quickly delayed Luchiriano's immediate plans.

By February, Vandal had gathered the ghouls remaining in the demon barrens and formed an army to fight the Noble Orc's forces.

A king normally remained safe in the base of operations, but Vandal had joined his envoys in directly visiting the ghouls and asking for their help. The effects of Death Attribute Allure had allowed him to smoothly gather the ghouls beneath his banner, but still . . .

"Am I a king or an errand boy?" Vandal mused.

"A king. You king. Oh, king. More ghouls mean more houses. Please make," said Vigaro.

"All right, all right."

Vandal used his Golem Creation skills to transform the shape of wood golems, along with a few other tricks to create more dug-out homes. It wasn't easy for him, with his general lack of architectural knowledge, but after living with the ghouls for more than a year, he could replicate their homes well enough. The materials to make them moved on their own, following his directions, and taking on the shapes he ordered them to, so golem housebuilding was actually pretty easy. So long as he had the materials, he could make one such house in less than ten minutes.

"Yes! Amazing! Make ten more!"

"King, make wall bigger too."

"Sure, sure." He turned more chopped wood into golems, and then formed it into lumber. Then he turned the ground into an earth golem and had it move aside, making a hole to form the dug-out house. He could make ten of these at the same time within the immediate surrounding area.

Once he reached the Olbaum Electorate Kingdom, he wondered if he could use this skill to make a living. He didn't know if they had any need of such dwellings, but he had the leeway to idly consider such a prospect while he worked.

After finishing another ten such homes, he moved on to the exterior wall. This was even easier than making the homes. All he needed to do was construct a sturdy wall. He could order the golems to move and then leave them in place, so it only took a few minutes.

"Impressive, king!"

"Lovely!"

"King, King, King!"

The ghouls were all chanting his title with their fists raised. The ghouls could be a somewhat slovenly race, so they were extremely appreciative of Vandal and his quick resolution of tasks that needed to be performed, even if they balked at following his example.

"Hey, Van. Your mother is calling for you."

"Okay. I'll leave the rest of this to you."

Vandal gave a bow and then departed. The ghouls continued their chanting for a while longer, happy to be free from doing the brunt of the work.

With the absorption of the four other grottos, including Talea's, the number of ghouls exceeded 270. Half of them were women, and some of them were elderly. But ghouls were a race that remained hardy warriors, male and female, until they were close to 200 years old.

The strongest ghouls joining them were some rank 4 Ghoul Warriors. They didn't get any new powerful additions of rank 5 or higher like Vigaro and Zadilis, but they also had Talea and her incredible equipment. This included Iron Turtle carapace armor, which boasted strength on par with full-plate armor but was far lighter, and a Lance Bull horn lance that could pierce steel armor. It was gear that even grade D adventurers would have trouble getting their hands on. They weren't magic items, but the strength of ghouls equipped with such equipment couldn't be measured purely by rank.

Humans were inferior to monsters in physical strength and special abilities, and so required three primary things in order to be able to defeat them, these being cooperation, skill, and equipment. The ghouls had now obtained the third one of these, but it came with a cost.

"You can't fight? At your age? You've lived ten times I have!" Basdia snapped.

"What of it? I've come this far by making gear and using my natural womanly weapons. A little girl who has never had a child should keep her mouth shut," Talea sniped back, the two of them glaring at each other.

One looked like a female warrior, well over six feet tall and in her mid-twenties, while the other looked like a small girl in her teens. The first was actually only a twenty-six-year-old girl, and the other a female leader who had lived a dramatic life for more than 260 years.

For some reason, the two of them didn't get along.

It was true, however, that Talea and the other women from her grotto didn't know how to fight. They didn't just lack combat skills—they had hardly learned any magic, which they should have had an aptitude for, outside of spells useful in everyday life. It would be hard for them to be of any help in battle.

However, Talea did have her women functioning as an organized group, which was rare for ghouls. None of them could match Talea, but they were still skilled at crafting gear, and they could help make more gear for the other warriors.

"Van is going to give me a child!" Basdia shot back.

"With a little girl like you?! Is this true, Lord Van?" Talea squawked.

Vandal sighed. "Not perhaps in the way you are thinking, but yes." He was talking purely about the resolution of the fertility problems. Vandal couldn't see why they were fighting.

"You need to stop being so friendly with Van," Basdia snapped.

"Me? You're the one who doesn't even call him 'lord'!" Talea countered.

The two of them continued to glare at each other. The sound of their gnashing fangs was extremely ghoulish.

They had been at each other's throats since Vandal returned with Talea and her ghouls. Talea had wanted to get into the Ghoul King's circle, and skillfully talked her way into the carriage to discuss the upcoming battle with him. When he drifted off into an infant-like nap, she had snuggled up with him, and that was how they had arrived at the grotto. Basdia had come out to greet them and found them like that, leading to an argument—and then to all this.

On reflection, Vandal did know the reasons. But the ghouls didn't have the concept of marriage, so he wasn't sure why Basdia was going so hard at Talea. It didn't seem like she was just being protective of a younger brother. He couldn't see why the pair of them were fighting so seriously over a two-year-old baby.

"Why don't you consider your age a little?" Basdia sniped.

"Oh, I'm sorry. Maybe because I was originally human, I tend to act the age I look," Talea replied. "I'm actually jealous of women like you. You're *so* mature-looking."

"For someone so young, those sure look saggy."

"Saggy?! Never! These aren't saggy. They're big! Big and bouncy!"

"Really? Mine don't point downward like yours."

Talea was losing her cool as she fought back, while Basdia was looking on and keeping her head. Both of them had incredible busts, and Basdia's did indeed point directly forward like missiles.

"You muscle-bound moron!" Talea shouted.

"You don't know? Van likes muscles."

"I'm not sure I'd say 'like'—more that I want them myself," Vandal offered. Muscles meant power, and power made someone strong; having muscles would allow him to cross the aisle and become one of the winners, not the downtrodden. *Sweet, sweet muscles.*

Maybe Basdia and Talea heard his comment, and maybe not, because they continued their fighting. The squawking Talea was unable to match the dispassionate Basdia, and the victory of youth over the wisdom of age seemed assured. Talea was unwilling to give up, however, so that victory was taking its sweet time to arrive. Vandal was looking forward to being able to constructively discuss how to handle the Noble Orc, but he had no idea when that was going to arrive.

"How can we put a stop to this?" he wondered aloud.

Zadilis was muttering about how they'd like to become an old lady without muscles or breasts, and Vigaro had his arms folded in deep thought, apparently. The other ghouls from Talea's own grotto were all subservient to her, meaning they couldn't weigh in.

You should step in and stop them, young master.

This came from Saria, as Sam was unable to move this far away from the carriage.

You want to become a noble, don't you? Then you need to be able to handle affairs like this.

"I think I need to reassess my expectations of being a noble," Vandal muttered.

Nobles always struggle with relationships with women. It was the same in the household where I worked, Saria replied. She said that the official wife and the concubine had always been at each other's throats. Vandal recalled similar such stories about women during the Edo period, when he was alive in Japan. Neither Basdia nor Talea were his wife or his concubine, but they were fighting over him, so he had to be the one to put a stop to it. He stood up.

"Hah! We'll settle this after one of my weapons has lopped off the head of the last Noble Orc!" Talea shouted.

"Yeah. After I've put your weapon to good use, then we'll settle this," Basdia countered.

In other words—everything was settled in the moment he stood up.

"Time to put together our strategy to handle the Noble Orc," he said. It was fortunate that he was able to keep his comments at that.

Their current combat strength was around 230 ghouls, plus Vandal and his little party. They were equipped with the magic items Vandal had provided and the gear created by Talea and her workforce. They were losing in terms of numbers, but their equipment was clearly a higher standard than what was used by the orc army. No matter the numbers of orcs, goblins, and kobolts under their command, it didn't make those monsters any smarter. Their equipment would only be slightly better than that of other packs of monsters.

Of course, there was no telling if those numbers alone would be enough to turn things around. Vandal had been planning to mass-produce golems and undead to help with the raw numbers, but the jungle suffered from a lack of the materials that would make the kind of Stone Golems and Rock Golems that could handle a bunch of orcs. Golems weren't going to work out as well as he had hoped.

When it came to undead, too, the rank 1 varieties freshly created from monster bones or corpses would be no match for orcs in terms of fighting strength, so that wouldn't work either. Increasing their number of living armor was another idea, as he could make that at rank 3, but it was a bigger boost to their fighting strength to put their armor onto their ghouls, so that idea was another non-starter.

They weren't making much progress.

"We have to be the ones launching the attack. That is for sure," Vandal asserted.

Everyone agreed. With the big numbers gap, even with a slight advantage in quality, they had to have initiative on their side. They were facing orcs, enemies relying on their raw, brute strength. Humans could build a sturdy fortress and try to defend against such a foe, but ghouls could not afford to go on the defensive. The wooden walls surrounding the grotto would only last a few seconds.

To put that another way, the orcs were bad at defending too.

"I already know their layout," Vandal said. "I've conducted recon through the eyes of my bug undead. It wasn't easy, but here's the resulting map."

He had only seen it all through the multifaceted eyes of bugs, so some of the details had escaped him, but it was enough to at least place the locations of buildings. The ghouls murmured in excitement at the map, which was drawn onto monster hide rather than paper.

"This map?"

"What this square?"

"Wow, Van. You drew this?"

"Lord Van, ghouls do not normally use maps. You will need to explain this in a little more detail," Talea said.

"Why did I work so hard on this?" Vandal muttered. He had been here two years, so he sometimes forgot the culture gap. He didn't dwell too long on the time he had spent creating the map, not wanting to get depressed. Instead, he turned the floor of the dug-out home into an Earth Golem and then used Golem Creation to make a model of the Noble Orc settlement. It looked pretty accurate, all things considered.

"Boy. If you can do this, why draw the map at all?" Zadilis asked.

Vandal made a dejected sound. Now he was depressed.

"Oh! Amazing!"

"Is this earth attribute magic? But I've never seen anyone command it with such precision!"

"This is even more amazing, Van! Much easier to under-stand than the map!"

All the onlookers preferred the model as well. Vandal decided he would skip the maps and just make models in the future.

"Moving on," Vandal said. "The wall surrounding the enemy settlement is comprised of uncut logs. There are two openings, in the east and west, and one watch tower located at each compass point. However, they are manned by kobolts and goblins."

"Orcs are heavy. They probably couldn't climb a scaffold," someone suggested.

The average orc was six feet in height and easily over 200 pounds. Weapons and armor only made them heavier. It wasn't that they didn't want to climb the watchtowers, but that they probably couldn't make watchtowers capable of supporting them.

"All the buildings are made of wood, in principle," said Vandal. "But we should avoid using fire as much as possible."

"Indeed," Zadilis agreed. "If it spreads too much, then the captured females will burn to death."

There were more than one hundred ghoul females and a few dozen female adventurers held in the settlement. The orcs needed them for breeding, of course, but they also wouldn't risk their lives in battle to protect them.

"In fact, they might use them as hostages," Vandal mused.

"A definite possibility," Zadilis agreed.

Vandal had never had to worry about the prospect of hostages before. But that was because he had been fighting with boney undead on the front lines. His foes would have presumed hostages to be meaningless. The main thrust of their forces this time would be ghouls, meaning the orcs would definitely consider using female ghouls as hostages.

"In that case, our first priority will be to capture these buildings at the rear," Vandal said.

They decided to save the captured ghoul females. Vandal had received numerous requests from the spirits of ghouls who were already deceased, and Zadilis and the others were of the mind that, if they were going to attack, they might as well save them. He couldn't oppose the line of thought.

"What about human female?" Vigaro asked.

"We'll save them too, if we can. We can work the other details out after we've saved them," Vandal replied.

Though also captives, female adventurers were still common enemies to the ghouls and Vandal. The adventurers might not feel especially grateful even if they were saved. From their perspective, it might seem like nothing more than switching captors from orcs to ghouls.

They might also try and use the chaos to escape or—in the worst-case scenario—launch an attack of their own. Vandal wasn't expecting that, however. The orcs wouldn't exactly have been giving them creature comforts. They weren't going to be in top mental or physical shape after being rescued and would be unlikely to move at all. Vandal also wanted to avoid giving the incoming cheaters any material to attack him with in the future.

"Charge in on Vandal signal and save female. Then kill enemy until they run. Sound good," Vigaro said.

"They are a group held together by nothing but fear," Vandal said. "Once a certain volume of orcs are wiped out, the goblins and kobolts should run for it."

"The Noble Orc only commands the lower orc race unconditionally," Zadilis added.

Most packs of monsters were held together by fear of the monster at the top. Encountering a source of greater fear could quickly make them fall apart. The orcs would remain under the control of the Noble Orc, their superior race. But Vandal needed the Noble Orcs to stick around. If they escaped, then the ghouls would be facing this exact same issue in a few years.

"Then Vandal back us up to kill Noble Orc," Vigaro said.

Vigaro was their strongest fighter. The suggestion was that, once buffed by Vandal, he would be able to handle the Noble Orcs, even if they were one or two ranks higher.

"Vigaro and Zadilis will take command, until the Noble Orc at the top reveals himself," Vandal said. "My party and I will fill in the gaps."

"I'm not sure about our king just filling in the gaps," Zadilis commented, "but that's the best way to apply your strength, boy. Make sure you have recon undead and ways to contact us prepared. You're the only one who can talk to the spirits."

Vandal had become the Ghoul King, but as he had said upon his appointment, he had no command skills. King or not, he was therefore best positioned as a flexible responder in this battle.

"Be careful, Van," Basdia told him. "Your life isn't just your own anymore."

"I know," he said. "Resolving the fertility issues relies on me. There's other things I want to do too."

He needed to learn some alchemy skills and resolve the ghouls' fertility issues. He wanted to try making walnut and acorn paste, and make a Mature magic item and a refrigerator using Whisp Fire prior to departing for the Olbaum Electorate Kingdom. There were many things he wanted to do for the ghouls, and many reasons to kill the Noble Orcs. He had to be careful and avoid getting too rash or reckless.

He also needed to complete his revenge and bring Dalshia back to life. He had plenty of reasons not to die.

"We'll set out in three days," he concluded.

Bzzzzz.

Countless bugs sped off to the east, east, east as fast as their wings would carry them.

Beetles, flies, dragonflies, wasps, ladybugs. Some of them would normally eat the others, but they flew on without heed to predator and prey relationships.

These bugs were the undead that Vandal had unleashed over a month previously, just as further insurance. He tasked them with finding another demon barren the ghouls could flee to if required, as well as to check out the path across the eastern mountains that Vandal was eventually hoping to cross.

Night and day, the bugs pushed on. Some were taken out by birds or other living bugs, but the survivors continued unabated. They crossed the mountains and pushed onward, past craggy rocks as sharp as knives and through scrub overgrown with carnivorous plants.

The bugs eventually stopped on part of a massive stone wall, located beyond one of the mountain ranges. It was big enough to be a mountain itself, although crumbling a little in places. They flew around for a while, and then settled on the wall.

They had completed their orders. Now they just had to wait here for their master to make contact. They would wait patiently until that time came.

Name: Skeleton
Rank: 3
Race: Skeleton Warrior
Level: 100
——Passive Skills
[Night Vision]
[Brute Strength: 2 (UP!)]
——Active Skills
[Sword Proficiency: Level 1] [Shield Proficiency: Level 1] [Bow Proficiency: Level 1]
[Sneaking Steps: Level 1] [Cooperation: Level 1 (NEW!)]

Name: Skeleton Bird
Rank: 3
Race: Phantom Bird
Level: 98
——Passive Skills
[Night Vision] [Spirit Body: Level 2 (UP!)] [Brute Strength: Level 2 (UP!)]
——Active Skills
[Sneaking Steps: Level 1] [High Speed Flight: Level 1]

Name: Sam
Rank: 3
Race: Ghost Carriage
Level: 65
——Passive Skills
[Spirit Body: Level 3 (UP!)] [Brute Strength: Level 3

(UP!)] [Off-Road Handling: Level 2 (UP!)]

[Resist Impact: Level 2 (UP!)] [Precision Driving: Level 3]

———Active Skills

[Sneaking Steps: Level 1] [Speed Driving: Level 1] [Charge: Level 2 (UP!)]

Name: Saria
Rank: 3
Race: Living One-Piece Swimsuit Armor
Level: 82
———Passive Skills

[Special Senses] [Physical Strength Enhancement: Level 2] [Resist Water Attribute: Level 2] [Resist Physical Attacks: Level 2]

———Active Skills

[Housework: Level 2] [Halberd Proficiency: Level 2 (UP!)]

[Bow Proficiency: Level 1 (NEW!)] [Cooperation: Level 1 (NEW!)]

Name: Rita
Rank: 3
Race: Living Bikini Armor
Level: 81
———Passive Skills

[Special Senses] [Physical Strength Enhancement: Level 2] [Resist Fire Attribute: Level 2] [Resist Physical Attacks: Level 2]

———Active Skills

[Housework: Level 1] [Naginata Proficiency: Level 2 (UP!)]

[Bow Proficiency: Level 1 (NEW!)] [Cooperation: Level 1 (NEW!)]

The large settlement ruled by the Noble Orc Bugogan was enjoying a peaceful night.

"Peaceful" being a relative term, of course, due to the screams of the captive women and the punishment of some goblins over a minor indiscretion by one of Bugogan's sons, Bubobio. But these were everyday occurrences, and so none of the monsters paid them much attention. They certainly weren't expecting anything out of the ordinary—such as an attack from another group of monsters.

In fact, in this settlement, peace was the norm. It was a settlement ruled by a Noble Orc, after all. When establishing a settlement in the demon barrens, weaker monsters like goblins and kobolts would generally select somewhere unlikely to be spotted by their enemies, such as caves or underground. Those led by a high-ranked monster could more afford to place their settlement above ground, where everyone could see, for the simple reason that they hardly had to worry about enemies of any kind.

Monsters had been created by the demon king and his evil gods after they arrived from another world. These creations were not interested in getting along with other monsters or anyone else. The different races would fight amongst themselves, even with each other, without batting a monstrous eyelid. However, those same monsters would never attack an opponent that was clearly more powerful than themselves. Even monsters knew not to commit suicide. They would never risk messing with a powerful Noble Orc, even by mistake. Other monsters could instinctively feel the presence of the powerful Bugogan and stayed well clear of his settlement.

In some very rare cases, the very lowest monsters who were unable to understand even that would ram into the exterior walls in an attempt to break them. That was why they had the watchtowers, which were posted with goblins and kobolts armed with bows.

The goblins guarding the towers grunted at one another. They didn't take their jobs especially seriously.

They were confident in their overall defenses. The exterior wall was a series of ten-foot logs driven directly into the ground. It was tougher than it looked and resistant to fire, because the wood had come from plant-based monsters called Ents. This provided defenses beyond those a stone wall could offer, including resisting the charge of a twenty-foot Mad Boar. Discussions of protecting the wall came a distant second among the goblins when compared to working out when the orcs would let them have some females again.

That, however, was a mistake.

Just before the moon reached its zenith, the supposedly impregnable exterior wall suddenly bulged with a terrible cracking noise.

The goblins scrambled for their bows in surprise, but there was nothing to shoot their arrows at. And yet all the logs comprising the wall continued to twist and bend. The goblins started to panic, unable to tell what was happening, as the exterior wall continued to warp.

With the sound of splitting, squealing wood, like the howls of vengeful spirits, the logs turned into wood golems.

All it took for the kobolt-constructed watchtower to crumble and collapse, and the goblins atop it to get smashed to the ground squealing, was their sturdy exterior wall—the wall that was meant to protect them from enemies—turning into those very enemies and starting to move.

The goblins should have been keeping better watch. But it was indisputable that doing so wouldn't have done them any good.

"First phase complete," Vandal confirmed with a nod. "The magical power had more difficulty penetrating the wood than I expected, but I've made the wood golems."

The wooden wall would have been very difficult to destroy by conventional means, but now it had effectively joined their side. This was the same trick he used when he turned the wall surrounding Evbejia into Stone Golems, except now he had the Magic Control skill, and his Golem Creation level had also increased, allowing the entire process to proceed far more efficiently.

"Although they aren't anything more than Wood Golems," Vandal admitted.

"It would still have taken us a long time to smash down that wall. You've saved us some time and allowed us to attack from all directions. A good start," Zadilis said. She was dressed in her combat gear, with a number of feathery decorations attached to her staff.

She was right—their preemptive attack was off to a great start. If the settlement had been nothing but goblins and kobolts, this alone might have been enough to settle matters.

But today, the main enemy they faced were orcs. Bellowing, wild orcs, closer to boars than pigs once the blood rushed to their porcine heads. Their own defensive walls turning into golems and attacking them would have thrown normal fighters into chaos, but the orcs were quick to respond to this abnormal situation. Without any orders, they took up heavy weapons and charged in, swinging their weapons around. It was an uncontrolled charge, but far more dangerous than them panicking or running around.

"Those Wood Golems are lasting longer than I thought," Vandal said.

"They're tougher than they look. Van, is this the strength of death attribute magic?" Basdia asked.

The ghouls didn't know the wooden wall was made from Ents, as tough as steel, and so they were surprised at how well the golems were holding up, figuring that was also the strength of Vandal's magic.

"Now then. Garrrrrr!"

Zadilis used the abbreviated language that the ghouls deployed during battle, her howl giving each unit the order to attack. The exact message was, "All units, attack! Eradicate the orcs, capture the target buildings, and secure the women!"

The other ghouls growled their own agreement, bearing their fangs and then charging into the settlement, now stripped bare without its wall.

The ghouls were outfitted with gear that would be the envy of grade D adventurers. They were also boosted with a range of support magic from their allied magicians, including Vandal and Zadilis. Ghouls and orcs were of similar strength, on a level playing field, but in terms of equipment, the ghouls were clearly ahead.

"Ghouuuuul!" Vigaro roared. He carried the biggest battle-axe among the ghouls and headed straight for an orc with a two-handed axe, which had just taken down a Wood Golem. The orc was wearing armor—simple armor, but still rare for an orc—indicating it was probably an Orc General. It was bulkier than a normal orc and raised its axe to face off with Vigaro.

With a shout, Vigaro thrust his shield forward. The orc grunted as its nose shattered, and then, when it staggered backward, Vigaro slashed a line across its exposed belly, spraying blood and entrails.

The Orc General was the same rank as Vigaro, 5. A clash between them would not normally end so easily. The difference came from daily training that wasn't reflected in level and rank, the effects of the support magic and Enhance Brethren skill, and above all else, the magic item battle-axe that Vandal had given Vigaro.

Although daily hard work, Enhance Brethren, and magic items would remain strong, the effects of support magic faded over time. Magicians needed to cast it again in order to prevent that from happening, but their MP wasn't infinite.

"Let me recover your magical power. Spirit Bodification."

That was where Vandal came in, with his MP that actually was close to being infinite. He used Spirit Bodification to turn both of his arms into spirit body, which then divided up like countless plant-like tendrils and connected to the bodies of all the ghoul's mages, including Zadilis.

"Urgh."

"Nngh . . ."

"Aaaahh!"

Each of them gave grunts or moans—one of them an especially big one. Vandal put the last of those out of his mind, and then unleashed the non-attribute magic that he had been learning since arriving in Zadilis's grotto.

"Magical Power Transfer!"

Among non-attribute magic, this was perhaps the least useful spell. It was magic that allowed non-attribute MP to transfer to someone else. At first glance, it might seem quite good. However, the majority of the transferred power was simply wasted. The transmission ratio depended on the relationship with the target, mental state, magical compatibility, and race, but the average was five percent. Twin magicians who trusted each other implicitly and had incredibly compatible magic had once recorded a seemingly impossible transfer rate of 200%—actually increasing the volume of transferred magic—but it was far more likely to cost more than it actually transferred. No method had yet been discovered to improve this transfer ratio. The upshot of this was that it was far more efficient to use the MP yourself than try to give it to other people. Using one hundred MP to transfer five was just silly.

Vandal, however, had more than one hundred million MP. If he had to spend 2,000 to give one hundred, or 20,000 to give 1,000, or 200,000 to give 10,000, very well. He could more than live with those numbers.

"That's turned the lights back on!" Vandal quipped. "This is the magical power version of a rich man burning money for candles!"

"Boy, I don't think gold or silver will burn very well," Zadilis said. "Regardless. Everyone, make good use of the MP he has provided you!"

"We will! Let's go, everyone!"

"We've got this!"

With their magic power boosted, the ghoul mages started off behind the warriors they were supporting. Vandal watched them go and then hopped up onto Sam, who was waiting at the side.

"Per our plan, we'll now begin our hit-and-run attacks, so please handle the rest," Vandal said to Zadilis. "You won't be able to see it, but I'll leave a familiar with you, so call on me if there's an emergency."

"Sure. You can leave it to me."

Vandal, the Ghoul King, was to bring the ghouls together with his Death Attribute Allure and enhance them with Enhance Brethren, then strike as required from Sam once the fighting started. He had no specific command capabilities, nor the capacity to see the entire battlefield. But he had death attribute magic like Magic Sucking Barrier, which could render the dangerous Orc Mages and other magic-using monsters worthless. The best way to make use of that was to launch guerilla attacks using Sam's superior mobility.

It still felt like the king was doing most of the heavy lifting, but Vandal's morale was actually high. After all, he was part of the strike force. They were always at the heart of the action, led by the hero, or with the hero among them. It was impossible for this development not to excite him.

"Sam, let's go," Vandal said.

At once.

The spirit body horse gave a whinny, and then Sam started out. Rita, Saria, and the skeleton were already in the carriage, with Skeleton Bear, Skeleton Bird, and the other undead outside, surrounding the carriage.

The strike force, who were definitely going to be the biggest thorn in the side of the Noble Orcs, joined the charge into the settlement.

Talea had remained behind, watching the ghoul warriors march out of the grotto with Vandal at their head. Now she was looking up at the sparkling stars in the night sky.

This was probably around the time they would be going into battle against the Noble Orcs. Talea had been informed of the details of the operation and had seen at least some of Vandal's incredible magical power. She had also provided them with all the gear that her own band of crafters could create. She had watched them leave, confident they had at least a seventy-percent chance of victory.

That said, in her 200 years of life, Talea had never experienced a battle on this scale. Even though she was pretty sure they could win, she still felt uneasy.

She knitted her fingers in front of her ample bosom and closed her eyes in prayer.

"I ask for victory for Lord Van and the others. I hope that Lord Van, my own warriors, Zadilis, Vigaro . . . and even that little minx Basdia will return safely. As many of them as possible."

She spoke aloud in prayer, putting her anxiety into words in order to stop it from knotting in her chest. When Talea opened her eyes again, Bildy and a number of other female ghouls were giving her incredulous looks.

"Talea," said Bildy. "You're praying not just for Vandal, but also our elder, and even Basdia? After all those arguments? You aren't a nasty person after all! I was sure you were!"

"You're just standing there saying all of this to my face, girl?! Those are the kinds of comments you should be muttering from the shadows! The rest of you too!" Talea exclaimed, her face red with embarrassment and anger, but Bildy and the other ghouls just looked at her, puzzled, not moving.

"I'm sorry," said another ghoul. "Bildy didn't seem to be able to sleep, so I was just coming out with her . . ."

"And we passed by you praying," Bildy said.

Talea looked at her again, taking in her swollen belly. She wasn't due yet, but she was getting close. Talea recalled being introduced to her as one of the pregnant ghouls from Zadilis's grotto, and proof that Vandal could resolve the fertility issue.

"Okay. If you've seen enough, go back to bed. Your baby doesn't want you walking around," Talea said.

She gave a sigh, still embarrassed, and then turned to go back to her own house. But Bildy called out for her to stop.

"I'm still not sleepy. Could we all talk for a while? I mean, you shouting like that kinda surprised me."

"I like your style, girl," Talea said. "Very well. I don't mind a little chat."

She had been planning on turning the girl down, but then recalled she couldn't sleep herself. She also realized that Bildy had to be pretty friendly with Vandal, if they had spent this much time together, and so decided to chat with her for a while.

"It sounds like you have something you specifically wish to discuss with me," said Talea, taking out her fan. "Go ahead, then. I'm listening."

Bildy needed no more prompting than that.

"I was wondering why you prayed for everyone to come back, and not just Vandal?" she asked.

"Especially Basdia, who you don't seem to get along with," chimed in another ghoul.

Bildy and the other ghouls had clearly noticed Talea's intentions to ingratiate herself with Vandal. That was why they were surprised at her praying so seriously for her rivals. But Talea just gave a shrug at the question.

"What do you expect? Even if the ghouls win this battle, losing too many warriors or magic users will cripple us going forward," Talea reminded them. "Even if Lord Van resolves the fertility problem, we can't replenish our numbers quickly like those goblins and kobolts can."

The maintenance of their settlements relied on those capable of combat—the ones who would hunt the monsters for food and gather other vital resources. It also took more than fifteen years for a ghoul to become a capable warrior. That meant that she didn't want to see their numbers decrease, even if she was from a different settlement.

Talea, in particular, was the leader of a settlement that had flourished due to trade with other grottos. It didn't matter how good her gear was if there weren't any warriors around to use it. Talea explained all this, and Bildy and the others looked quite impressed.

"You have more common sense than I expected, Talea. I thought you were a stranger person than this."

"You seem to have a strange opinion of me."

The others muttered their agreement with Bildy, at which Talea's fan quivered for a moment.

"Enough of this, or when Lord Van returns, I'll beg him to punish you!"

"Now you sound like a spoiled child," Bildy said. "It's just you are a bit odd, Talea. Your hair, that fan, even the way you talk."

She could be forgiven for having that impression too. Talea's side ringlets hairstyle wasn't something the other ghouls had seen before. What they could tell, from even just a glance, was that it took a lot of work and time to maintain.

Then there was Talea's fan. This demon barren looked like a jungle, but it actually wasn't all that hot or steamy. There was no need for the fan outside of maybe summer. It was currently winter, and yet she was walking around with that fan, showing it off or using it to cover her mouth. And her imperious tone spoke for itself.

For Bildy and the others, living a life of hunting and gathering in the demon barrens, everything Talea did looked strange and unnecessary.

"None of the ghouls in my grotto say things like this!" Talea exclaimed.

"I guess they're used to you by now," Bildy said, hitting upon the truth of the situation. In addition to that, the ghouls in Talea's grotto and those around it knew she was originally human. So when she did something a little strange, they just chalked it up to differences from her human culture or values.

"This is why you grottos that don't trade with me have such limited scope of vision! You need to open your eyes to the wider world!"

"Yes, we will! Sorry!"

"In that regard, this situation does provide you with an opportunity," Talea said. "A chance to meet some new ghouls."

Bildy and the others all nodded meekly, perhaps seeing her point. They might have found Talea to be a strange ghoul, but they didn't dislike her.

"You young ghouls, I don't know what to do with you sometimes. Aren't you worried that Lord Van and the others aren't going to make it back safely?"

This question, coming from a ghoul who had lived for more than 200 years, did take the slightly more scatterbrained Bildy and other young ghouls a little by surprise.

"Of course we're worried, but they have Vandal with them. They should be fine," Bildy said. "His strength is impossible to measure by our usual standards."

"We've never seen anyone stronger than Elder Zadilis or Vigaro," another ghoul admitted, "so it's difficult for us to imagine these Noble Orcs."

It turned out, then, that Talea had been right—these ghouls only knew a small slice of the world. And yet they had Vandal pegged as bizarre, even with that general lack of understanding.

With the status, skills, and ranks that existed on Ramda, differences in strength were often clearly represented as numerical values. In principle, the bigger the difference between those numbers, the bigger your advantage—or disadvantage—would be. As that gap grew larger, it became harder and harder for things like strategy or luck to turn the situation around.

In Vandal's case, however, it wasn't just about having more than one hundred million MP. It was also the fact that his powers were completely unknown. He could talk to spirits, create undead and golems, detect the potential for death, and had a skill that made him so appealing to ghouls he had gathered all the grottos under his banner—including Talea's—with relative ease. All of these were things that no ghoul had ever seen before. They were complete unknowns, as they were to the Noble Orcs. The attack that had been launched, in which Vandal would play a key role, would surely be full of surprises for them.

After living with him for more than a year, Bildy and the others believed Zadilis and the others were going to win, led to victory by their Ghoul King Vandal.

"Although they did keep assuring us that they were going to win before they left. That makes me a little uneasy," Bildy admitted.

"In our condition, they probably didn't want us upsetting ourselves," said another, "but they went a little far with it."

Without any solid proof for claims of a complete victory, those assurances rang a little hollow. That was probably why Bildy had been unable to sleep on this particular night.

"She's got thirty years on me! She shouldn't be making mistakes like that. Although I probably put some fuel on that fire," Talea said. "How about you enjoy a change of pace by joining me in praying for their safe return? Come on, pray with me. It should help to calm you down a little."

Talea closed her fan and knitted her fingers again, ready to pray.

Gods actually existed in this world. So prayer was widely believed to reach them. The rare skill Angel Advent allowed the user to become a messenger of the gods themselves, and there were numerous tales of gods making miracles happen at the behest of heroes or the maidens who looked up to them.

Of course, such occurrences were rare, and were often considered to be old fables or the result of rare skills. Talea had been sold off as a slave by her own family, so she wasn't really expecting her prayers to make a miracle happen. The main thing she was counting on was the mental effect of reducing her anxiety.

"Okay. For now we can only wait and pray." Bildy put her hands in front of herself and also started to pray. "Lady Vida, our ancestors, I ask you. Please, protect them."

That was when Talea realized she hadn't actually selected a target for her own prayers. She had been praying to an indeterminate "god," nothing else.

When she was human, she had belonged to the Alda faith, like everyone else around her. Now that she was a ghoul, she presumed she should be praying to Vida. She took her lead from Bildy and repeated the same prayer as her. Even after she finished, however, Bildy alone kept praying.

"I can sense your passion," Talea told her, "but don't overdo it or you won't be able to calm down."

"Please, bring them back safely—I know, but I absolutely want Vandal to come back alive," Bildy replied, completing her prayers and placing her hands on her belly. "I want him to be godfather to my child . . . and once he's all grown up, I'm going to want this little one to have a brother or sister."

"Hold it! Hold on a moment!" There were words in there that Talea couldn't overlook, and her voice rose. "This godfather business is one thing, but what does having another child have to do with anything?"

"Huh?" Bildy looked surprised. "Isn't it obvious? Once Vandal is older, he's going to father a child for me. I bet his kids would be really strong—although he'll probably have left to live with the humans by then."

Talea stiffened with shock at this reply from Bildy. She had her own plans to ingratiate herself with Vandal to improve her own circumstances, so Bildy's revelations had a serious impact on her. Talea had known about Basdia, but hadn't expected Bildy to have a similar plan. The first half of her statement had surprised her so much that Talea hadn't even registered the second half.

"Someone else, waiting in ambush, another one . . . I'm sorry, I don't feel very good."

With that, Talea staggered away toward her house.

Bildy and the others called out goodnight behind her, but it fell on deaf ears.

The shock kept Talea up almost the rest of the night. Bildy, meanwhile, returned to her own house and fell right asleep.

The Death Mage

CHAPTER THREE

GHOULS VS. ORCS!

For the orcs—and in particular for their leader Bugogan—it was completely unexpected to be on the receiving end of a raid. They were the attackers, not the attacked. That was mainly because they didn't share information about themselves with the ghouls and humans who could potentially do them harm.

So they only put the low-morale goblins and kobolts up on the watchtowers. The orcs spent their time sating their sexual desires with the captive women or just sleeping the days away.

The sounds of the Wood Golems trashing their settlement and the screams of the goblins and kobolts woke those orcs up, sending them into a panic. Rather than wait for orders from their superiors, they started to fight back on their own. An Orc General who had happened to be on the perimeter tried to gather the orcs, but Vigaro chopped him down with a single attack.

This further escalated the panic of the orcs, and that trickled down to the slave goblins and kobolts. There was no hope of them acting in an organized fashion. In fact, the orcs, wildly swinging around their sticks and axes, were taking out as many allies as enemies.

The kobolts were the first to recover from the panic. They were comparatively smart and good at cooperating, so around a core of Kobolt Chiefs and Kobolt Mages, they avoided engaging the Wood Golems and focused on countering the ghouls.

"Graaaaaah!"

The ghoul combat unit led the charge. They used their long arms to gallop like gorillas into the settlement. With their lion-like faces, they looked almost comical, but thanks to their magic-enhanced Brute Strength, their charge was as fast as that of military horses.

"Arf arf!"

The kobolts whined at the incoming speed, perhaps getting in a single arrow. Such attacks were rendered ineffective by the light but tough armor provided by Talea and the support magic from Zadilis and her mages. The kobolts' whining only intensified as the ghouls closed in and started using their claws to slash down their foes one after another. Even the Kobolt Chief, ostensibly in command, was cut down without offering any meaningful resistance.

The ghouls roared back, splashed with the blood of their kills, and pushed deeper into the settlement. To humans, they might have looked like nothing more than blood-thirsty beasts, but those who understood the ghoul combat language would have known they were shouting, "We've come to save you!" These were warriors, here to save the captive women.

Young master. We have a group of goblins ahead.

"Ram—"

Very well! Ramming speed!

The carriage, pulled by its pale horse, sped through the orc settlement. Its frame was enhanced with spikes made from the fangs of monsters, allowing it to charge more like a chariot.

That sight already carried a significant impact, but even more terrifying was Sam, the driver. His eyes were wide open, sparkling bloodred, and his teeth formed a terrible leer from his pale face.

Goblin Soldiers and Knights had shields and spears up to try and push the carriage back, but their grunts of exertion quickly changed to screams as the wagon rolled right over them. They were punctured by the spikes, caught up in the wheels, and quickly ground to dust.

Normally the carriage itself would also take some damage, but it had been enhanced with extensive use of parts made from Ent wood, so it didn't even take a single scratch.

Hahaha! I really am enjoying this, young master!

Father, don't get too carried away.

Go! Go, go, go!

I can't stop myself!

The craftier ghouls under Talea had greatly upgraded the carriage that served as Sam's body, using all sorts of materials from monsters. It had felt a little like turning a human into a cyborg without using any anesthetic, but Sam had made assurances that more than ninety percent of his parts could be safely swapped out, so long as he retained the form of a carriage. Vandal himself had been replacing the bones that got broken or cracked on his skeleton undead, but even he hadn't expected them to safely be able to completely replace so much of Sam.

The results of these modifications were a serious increase in combat strength, even while remaining a rank 3 monster.

Young master! Now we have orcs in front of us!

There were three of them, snorting through their noses with axes and poles at the ready. These were rank 3 enemies, the same rank as Sam, and each of them was over 100 kilograms in weight, making them much bigger and heavier than goblins.

They had piggy faces and flabby-looking bodies, but beneath that, they had powerful, thick muscles protecting their bones and organs, and the bones themselves were far harder than human ones.

Saria and Rita fired off arrows powered up by Vandal with Lethality Enhancement, but they were unable to pierce the wall of fat and muscle. In the end, they only further angered the orcs. Thanks to the magic, the arrows must have done some damage, but they certainly didn't have any visual effect.

Vandal opened his mouth to suggest that they try to circumvent the orcs. "Safety first—" he started.

Very well! Safety first as I roll right over them! Sam responded.

Vandal wanted to try and stop him, but Sam accelerated before the infant could speak again.

The orcs snarled as they launched battle techs, with the intention of slaying the incoming three horses and then smashing the carriage that was following behind.

Flicker Slash, Cleave, and Two Tier Thrust: all level 1 battle tech that newbie adventurers could use, but the Brute Strength of the orcs propelled them to incredible levels of damage. Or *should* have, if they were fighting corporeal enemies.

Their assortment of pointy weapons just passed right through the pale horses, like nothing more than sticks through viscous mud.

The orcs grunted and howled, thrown off balance by the lack of impact, and then their brief and brutal lives came to an end when they bounced like rubber balls out from underneath Sam's charging body.

The three horses pulling the carriage were pale, but at a glance they looked like normal horses. In reality, they manifested as a part of Sam's Spirit Body skill, astral-type monsters that were almost completely unaffected by physical attacks. Whacking at them with lumps of forged steel, no matter how hard, would have zero effect.

The orcs had no idea. Unbalanced in the attempted attack, they couldn't hope to avoid Sam's charge.

This is wonderful! Simply wonderful! I feel my strength growing with each life I crush! Sam exclaimed.

"Ah, you're earning experience. Good. I don't mind that at all, but please try to drive safely," Vandal admonished.

Very well!

Sam was normally an affable gentleman, but each jolt of experience cast further light into his pupils . . . indeed, into the entirety of his eyeballs.

People are always so surprising, Vandal thought. Sam's daughters were shouting about how cool he looked, so Vandal wasn't going to complain. Still—could a luxury limo and a murder death tank coexist in the same vehicle? Vandal was caught for a moment on the prospects for Sam's future before Skeleton Bird let out a screech that caught his attention.

"Gaaaaah!"

"Awooooo!"

Skeleton Bear used its own Brute Strength to disembowel one orc, while Skeleton Wolf weakened another with Poison Breath before Skeleton Monkey finished the job.

All his undead were pulling their boney weight. The flying Skeleton Bird was reporting the movements of the orcs below, allowing the undead on the ground to pinpoint the orc commanders and keep the enemy panicked and confused.

"Our forces are rolling right over them," Vandal muttered.

He had the leeway to take in the scene and comment in this fashion because the spirits of the enemies killed in the slaughter were flocking to him in droves.

It wasn't just the ones killed by Sam and the other undead. There were spirits killed by Vigaro, Basdia, and the other ghouls. He estimated there were nearly 200 of them. That meant they had already killed more than half of the enemies. Meanwhile, there wasn't a single spirit from among his allies. The enemy forces had lost fifty percent of their strength, while his allies were untouched. If they had been fighting humans, there was no way for their enemies to come back from this. Victory would have been assured.

"But we're dealing with a horde of monsters," Vandal said. "The Noble Orcs haven't appeared yet either. I think it's time to put my Lemures to work."

Sam raced freely around the settlement. Their allies were all in good shape. They had already captured the building where the female ghouls were held captive. But the Noble Orc behind it all still hadn't appeared yet. This concerned Vandal, so he decided to put into action another of the tricks from his training with Zadilis—Lemures.

Each attribute magic could use magical power to create familiars. These were formed from attribute-enhanced MP and followed the commands of the one who created them, like remote drones powered by magic. Familiars' abilities and strengths depended on their creator. They generally took the form of small animals, and included everything from butterflies made of fire to birds made of wind. The form Vandal had selected was a flying skull.

The freshly created Lemures groaned, assuming the form of a nearly transparent skull. It had all the normal functions of a familiar, such as sharing its five senses with its master, in addition to being incredibly difficult to spot.

"Graaaaah! Groooooh!"

An Orc General had just appeared in front of them, with some Orc Knights. Vandal decided to put it to the test at once.

Young Master. Should I avoid this encounter? Sam asked.

The orcs had shields up, just like the goblins from before, but it would be foolish to equate the two. Sam kept his cool and asked for confirmation.

Vandal simply told him to charge all the same.

Very well! Sam initiated a third charge forward.

The Orc General had a piggy smile on his face as he saw what was happening. He had his own Shield Bash skill, which could send a rampaging fifteen-foot Mad Boar flying, plus an Orc Knight standing on both sides of him. The carriage charging toward them was going to get smashed to splinters, nothing more. The Orc General had absolute confidence as he and his two minions moved to activate Shield Bash at the same time . . . and then he paused. He felt a terrible presence—a lethal desire to kill, coming from directly behind them.

The Orc General and his Orc Knights were seized by a primal animal terror—that if they didn't act at once, they would immediately be killed. They spun around on the spot, turning their shields toward this terrifying new enemy.

But there was nothing there to turn around to.

The overwhelming terror was gone too, leaving the orcs puzzled and confused—and then howling in pain as Sam arrived and ran them down.

They might have powerful defenses and charging strength, but that meant nothing if they were facing away with their shields down. The wagon rolled right over them.

The general was still alive, barely, but it was rank 5. It tried to stagger back onto its feet, but that wasn't going to happen either.

"Sam, stop," Vandal ordered. "Reverse."

Very well! The wheels that had crushed the Orc General started to rotate in the opposite direction, and the carriage halted before beginning to accelerate again—backward.

"Hrrgh?!"

Piggy eyes bulging in disbelief, the orc was run over a second time and finally killed.

The terror the orcs had felt, which had instinctively made them turn around—that was the power of the Lemures.

The familiar unleashed a powerful intent to kill that appealed directly to the lizard brains of its targets, before vanishing on the spot. That was all it could do. It had no actual attacks. It might be able to cause a heart attack in the old and frail. Maybe. In peacetime, it was little better than a prank.

But during combat, there were few better distractions. Even better, the more sensitive the target was to threats on their life, the more effective it became.

"If I had been able to make these on Origin . . ." Vandal mused. "No, I doubt that would've changed anything." He needed to stop looking into the past and consider the present.

Still aboard Sam, Vandal started to race around the roads of the settlement, which had been created to accommodate the orcs' broad sizes, to pinpoint the more intelligent among the monsters, such as the Goblin Mages, Kobolt Mages, and

Orc Mages, and use Magic Sucking Barrier to completely nullify them.

At the same time, he scattered Lemures out across the settlement, using them to back up the ghouls while also preparing for the appearance of the Noble Orcs. Less than a minute later—

"Noble Orcs are about ten feet tall, with golden hair, correct?"

That is what I have been told, Sam replied.

"Then I've found them," Vandal said. "Three of them, all at once."

One of them was standing in front of Vigaro as the ghoul continued his rampage. Another was heading for Zadilis and the unit at the rear. And the third was heading for Basdia and the warriors.

All three of them looked even bigger and tougher than the Orc General they had just rolled over, and had golden hair that gleamed in the moonlight.

These had to be the sons of the Noble Orc who ruled this settlement. The Kobolt Shaman had warned that they were rank 6, far stronger than any Orc General—and even stronger than any of the ghouls, including Vigaro and Zadilis.

"Skeleton Monkey, Skeleton Wolf, Skeleton Bear, and Skeleton Bird, you protect Zadilis and support the Lemures," Vandal ordered. "Sam, head for Basdia."

For yet another night, Luchiriano was unwillingly watching the Noble Orcs through his Living Dead.

He honestly wanted to head to the Olbaum Electorate Kingdom right away, but so long as the Living Dead remained intact, Luchiriano would continue to share its senses in service of Viscount Valchez. Luchiriano received an emergency designated quest from the viscount, and had hardly been able to turn down a bag stuffed with gold.

But this is torture! The viscount and the adventurers' guild are working to destroy any virtue left in my heart!

It was the perfect showcase for Luchiriano's unique life attribute magic, capable of collecting further information with zero risk to himself or others. He should have jumped at the chance, but there was a simple reason why he was finding it so distasteful.

Luchiriano had turned a fresh female corpse he had received from Viscount Valchez into the latest Living Dead. And the Noble Orc Bugogan had taken quite an unholy liking to it.

Luchiriano had learned the orc tongue, and he had let out a yelp of true horror when he heard Bugogan say, "I will give this female adventurer the glory of birthing my fourth child."

Sharing his senses with the Living Dead meant that he got to experience the "glory" of the Noble Orc from a front-row seat. It was visual violence. Worse—a waking nightmare.

The world was a big place, and while there were some who got off on the idea of seeing beautiful women being defiled by beasts or monsters, he had never heard of anyone wanting this vision filled with the face of a grunting, ugly orc. Luchiriano himself might have gone by the alias "The Depraved," but he certainly didn't have such tastes himself. He could only survive it because the Living Dead provided hardly any tactile sensations, and a very reduced sense of smell.

Still, I have learned a lot of information, Luchiriano thought. *Monsters are no exception to letting their mouths run away with them in the bedroom.*

Bugogan completely dropped his guard when he was around the Living Dead controlled by Luchiriano. That made sense. The Living Dead hardly reacted at all, offering neither resistance nor anger, and to the orc was nothing more than a machine to give him another child. So simply talking to himself, he shared all his complaints about daily life and even his resentment for the Noble Orcs from his home with her.

Luchiriano passed on all of this information with the viscount, providing further lubrication to his purse.

That night, Luchiriano was debasing himself again, looking up at Bugogan from inside the Living Dead and hoping for more comments that would make this all worthwhile, when an orc who acted as servant for the leader burst into his chamber.

It seemed that the settlement was under a full-scale attack.

There is a lot of ambient noise tonight, Luchiriano thought, *but I thought it was just drunken orcs. I guess not.*

The attack had been launched by a large army of ghouls, and the situation was not going well. Numerous Orc Generals had already been slain, and the number of Orc Mages reduced.

"Bugaaah! Bugigi, Bubobio!"

Bugogan raged at the damage to the forces he had spent so long to create. He ordered Bubobio and his other sons into action and then climbed off the Living Dead. He appeared to be going into battle himself.

I need to let the viscount know about this. The ghouls would surely lose in the end, but they would do serious damage to the Noble Orc's forces first. That would put off their plans to attack in the spring or summer.

With the orcs' reduced strength, they might not need one hundred or more adventurers. A party of two of grade B might be able to take care of the problem. *I'd love it if the Living Dead gets destroyed too!*

Then he could take the money and run, heading off on his own journey. As though rising to meet those expectations, the sounds of fighting were only getting louder from outside Bugogan's house.

"Raaagh! Pig-headed cowards! No one brave enough to face me?!" Vigaro shouted, his mane bristling, his teeth bared as he roared.

The orcs and goblins he was facing probably didn't understand what he was saying, but they still backed down in fear.

Vigaro's role in this battle was distraction. He was clearly high ranking among the ghouls and had ten other warriors with him, including magicians. His rampage certainly caught the attention of the enemy. That allowed Basdia and the others to move in and save the women. Humans would have immediately seen through the deception, with the execution being far from skillful. But this was all it took to fool a bunch of monsters.

Monsters were all very aggressive. They couldn't help but focus their attention on Vigaro and his rampaging party, killing so many of their allies within their own territory. Orcs were a particularly aggressive race, and when generals or other commanders appeared, they were immediately defeated by Vigaro, meaning there was no bringing the monsters under control.

A rare type of orc, an Orc Tamer, appeared, bringing a Wood Wolf, Huge Boar, Giant Python, and other monsters, but the ghouls defeated them with ease. They were pathetically weak compared to the undead Vandal had with him.

Orc General easy to kill now, Vigaro thought. *Same rank as me, but easy. We stronger? Vandal made stronger.*

Vigaro had the effects of the Enhance Brethren skill and the magic battle-axe. There was also all the support magic, which was being sustained by Vandal and his magical power Transfer keeping everyone's MP topped off. Furthermore, when the Orc Mages and Goblin Mages who would normally give the ghouls trouble appeared, Vandal unleashed black mist somewhere in the vicinity, enclosing that mage and sealing off their magic. The result was that not one of their allies had been seriously hurt. In fact, they hadn't suffered even minor injuries.

Vigaro had mixed feelings about relying so heavily on the child, but ghoul society had always been predicated on strength. The most powerful should naturally rise to the top, and Vigaro knew that Vandal was, ultimately, above him.

In terms of pure muscles and physical strength, Vigaro was definitely ahead. In terms of battle techniques, he was ahead too. But in terms of magic and magical power, it was clearly Vandal. More than anything else, the one with the Enhance Brethren skill should be at the top. Vandal met all the conditions to rise to the top, so that was where he was.

I chief of one hundred ghoul. Vandal chief of me. That was how Vigaro accepted the situation, but he still felt a bit pathetic— purely from the standpoint of being worthy to serve Vandal, or rather, to be one of his family.

That was why, when he heard the roar of rage that surpassed that of any Orc General, Vigaro's mouth lifted at both corners.

The source of such rage was a young but massive Noble Orc, seemingly carved from nothing but arrogance and ugliness apart from his golden hair, and large enough to make the six-foot-plus Vigaro look small His eyes burned with rage at Vigaro from ten feet off the ground. His thoughts on the situation were clear. He had come to punish these weaklings, whom his own minions seemed so incapable of doing anything about.

"Noble Orc!"

"Vigaro! What now?"

Even the elite ghouls were unable to hide their uncertainty. Orc Generals were on the same level as Vigaro, but this was clearly something superior. The rank 5 Ghoul Barbarian Vigaro might have only been one number before the rank 6 Noble Orc, but that was a big gap to fill. In a fight between two monsters, head-on and with both in reasonable condition, the higher rank would almost always win unless some element of the matchup disadvantaged the one with the higher number. A fox couldn't hope to fight a tiger head-on and win, regardless of its experience or skills. Vigaro had himself stated that he would lose if he had to fight this enemy.

"What now? We fight!" Vigaro shouted. He certainly didn't feel like they could lose! He gave a lion's roar, and closed in with the Noble Orc. The orc looked down on him from above, and then swung his own axe—which was twice the size of the one Vandal had given to Vigaro—in a brutal horizontal slice.

The attack would have taken Vigaro's head off, had it connected, but he avoided it by dropping down to the ground.

His anger flared as the axe trimmed some of his mane off, but rather than let that get the better of him, he used three of his limbs to propel himself sideways.

"Hrrgh!"

But the axe, which should've passed overhead, was now coming straight at him.

Axes were normally poorly balanced weapons, requiring some time to adjust one's stance after each swing before being able to attack again. It was normally impossible to attack again immediately. But the Noble Orc had the strength to make that possible.

Grunting madly, the orc unleased an axe combo that was based not on technique but raw strength. It looked at a glance to leave the orc wide open for an attack, but if Vigaro bit, he would have been reduced to bloody ribbons in seconds.

Instead, he continued to dance lightly between the attacks. He still had his own axe in one hand while using his other hand and both legs to grab the ground, push himself off it, and avoid the Noble Orc's blows.

The force of each incoming attack was monumental, swinging in at incredible speeds powered by the orc's muscles. But the movements were also straightforward and wildly telegraphed. From Vigaro's perspective, it was like the orc was standing there and explaining each of his attacks before he made them.

"Grah!"

"Hrrrgh!"

"Raagh!"

Meanwhile, the warriors in the respective entourage of each combatant joined the fray. Vigaro was following the situation with his understanding of the ghoul battle language, but the Noble Orc was completely fixated on the ghoul in front of him.

He simply couldn't work out why his attacks weren't hitting! He was Bugiblio, the strongest son of his mighty and powerful father! He was unable to comprehend how a mere ghoul could avoid all of his attacks so easily.

Ghouls were nothing to a Noble Orc, nothing more than meat waiting to be slaughtered! And yet, here he was, suffering this humiliation in front of all of his underlings and slaves.

"Bugaaaaaaaaaaaaaaaah!" he roared.

Anger overtook Bugiblio, and he unleashed the battle tech Cleave. It was at level 2, making it strong enough to chop clean through a tree even when used by a human; when used by a Noble Orc, it could crush boulders.

However, that increased strength meant larger, more obvious movement, and a bigger opening after the attack was complete. Vigaro not only avoided the attack but seized the resulting opportunity to counterattack.

"Whip Axe!"

Vigaro's long arm thrashed out like a whip. The pig grunted, attempting to avoid the sudden counter, but Vigaro immediately thrashed out again, sinking his axe deep into the right arm of the Noble Orc.

The orc howled in agony, but Vigaro wasn't finished yet. He released the haft of his battle-axe with his right hand, and then grabbed it from the air with his left.

Then, he unleashed his battle tech again.

"Hrk, hrkaaaargh!"

The axe closed in on the orc's neck. The orc attempted to block the attack with his own axe, but as Vigaro's axe rebounded away, Vigaro whipped his arm in the opposite direction, cleaving off the Noble Orc's undefended right leg.

The orc tumbled to the ground and placed his head on the figurative chopping block—and this time, Vigaro's axe bit deeply into the piggy creature's neck before lopping his head right off.

He had used Whip Axe, which made full use of ghouls' highly flexible arms, and the combo attack Triple Whip Axe. These were battle techs that were passed down solely among the long-armed ghoul males.

Vigaro gave a triumphant roar. "Who's next?!" he bellowed.

At the terrifying sight of Vigaro stamping down on the Noble Orc's head, still frozen in a death scream, the morale of the orcs crumbled away to screaming of their own, and they started to scramble to get away.

But there was no escape for the slow and bulky orcs. It wasn't long before they too were following their master, just as the goblins and kobolts had already done.

"Ghouuuul! Well, Vandal? See? Family strong!"

The child had called them family. He had not only joined in this battle—a battle he didn't need to have anything to do with—but accepted the name of king. And now he was working harder than any of them. Vigaro could hardly call himself a chief, hardly a warrior, if he couldn't prove himself to Vandal.

Vigaro continued to shout proudly as blood rained down around him.

"Someone saw through Vigaro's distraction."

When the group of orcs appeared, led by the Noble Orc equipped with a bow, Zadilis muttered to herself.

She was facing five Orc Knights equipped with shields and seemingly in position to protect the Noble Orcs, five additional orcs equipped with mighty clubs and leather armor, and maybe thirty goblins with daggers and short spears. It was hardly an army, considering the numbers, but having a Noble Orc among them made all the difference.

"Elder, we should fall back," a ghoul suggested.

Zadilis had been hoping their momentum would continue to propel them forward, but the ghouls had sweat on their brows and looked ready to cut and run.

"Everyone, stand firm!" Zadilis shouted. "If you have the time to voice such concerns, give voice to your magic instead, and bolster our warriors! They will surely come to our aid!" Zadilis felt fear of her own in the face of the Noble Orc, but she chose fight rather than flight. The main reason for that was because their foe was clearly underestimating them.

Vandal was out there, fighting on his own, but he was using bug undead and the Lemures to watch the entire battle. If the enemy weren't taking this threat seriously, Zadilis and her magic users could hold out until Vandal realized what was happening and came to help.

The Noble Orc with the bow—Bugogan's youngest child, Budibis—casually looked on as the comments from Zadilis removed the fear from the ghouls and restored the fight to their eyes.

Budibis grunted. When he had heard the report of a group comprised almost entirely of females, he planned to capture them alive. He could find one or two for himself and present the rest to his father, allowing him to get a leg up on his brothers. That had been the extent of his thinking on the matter.

But these females looked hardened. Ready to fight. The one in the front looked just right for a proud warrior such as himself. She was a little small, and didn't have much meat on her, but he could overlook such minor shortcomings.

"Buhoho, bufururubu! Bukyu!" He grunted out his orders, letting his minions know that the commanding female was his, and that they should capture her alive.

Following his orders, the orcs with the clubs formed in a horizontal line and prepared to charge.

Zadilis knew what Budibis was thinking: they were planning to break the ghouls' front line, then send in the light-footed goblins to maintain the pressure, while Budibis picked off enemies with his bow from afar. It wasn't hard to read his piggy plan. She shuddered as his gaze crawled over her body again, and then she used the guttural ghoul combat language to give fresh orders to her allies.

In that moment, the orcs started their charge. They were putting everything they had behind the strength of their charge, seeking simply to scatter the ghouls.

"Sunblind!"

Zadilis unleashed light attribute magic, burning the eyes of the incoming orcs. All it did was flicker a blinding light, but it almost completely wiped out the vision of the charging orcs. Two of them tripped and hit the ground, squealing as they fell, but the remaining three continued their charge forward even though they couldn't see.

"Eat this! Stone Shot!"

"Steel Claws! Gaaaah!"

The spells from the other ghouls focused on the remaining three orcs. Stones, fire, and lightning crackled down onto their legs and faces, eliciting more screams. Claws from the defending ghoul warriors also struck the orcs, sending them sprawling with blood spurting everywhere.

The goblins came next, leaping over the fallen orcs like chattering monkeys. Zadilis had hoped they would lose their nerve after seeing the orc charge stopped in its tracks. At least the goblins didn't have any generals or knights among them—just rank 2 soldiers. Zadilis's unit wasn't skilled at close combat, but they could handle this.

"Hrgh!"

Then Budibis unleashed an arrow. The powerful arrow, carved from an Ent branch, closed in on one of the ghoul warriors.

"Wind Shield!"

Zadilis barely had time to get her wind attribute magic off, and just managed to deflect the arrow. The ghoul warrior took it in the arm rather than the chest, and still got knocked back, but ghouls were very resistant to pain. He was back on his feet almost immediately.

Budibis nocked another arrow with an affected pose, unconcerned by the lack of impact of his first attack. He gave a piggy chuckle, secure in his confidence that victory was assured.

This small number of warriors would not be able to stop all of his minions, and the magicians wouldn't be able to kill the orcs by themselves. Zadilis, who should have been giving commands, was caught up in preventing his arrows from finding targets. In a few moments, Zadilis and the other female ghouls would run out of MP. Once that happened, it'd be like taking candy from a baby.

His slave goblins and the orcs that had charged in there might get wiped out, but they could make more so long as they captured these females.

This was truly a noble battle. Let the grubby minions clash, covered in blood and gore, while he elegantly shot down his foes from afar. He had truly refined battle to its most elegant essence. Something his brothers couldn't do, of course. Not even his father could do this.

"Hurk hurk hurk!" he chuckled, even as his second and then third arrows were also blocked. To him, they were nothing more than a countdown to victory. Budibis took a moment to imagine the moment Zadilis would become his, as she stood there, sweat on her skin, desperately chanting her spells.

However, when his fifth arrow was also blocked, Budibis realized something was wrong. Zadilis's magic was not fading, not losing its power as he had expected it to.

He snapped back from his daydreaming to examine the state of the battle, and the magic unleashed by the ghoul mages had already wiped out most of the goblins and orcs.

Three of his Orc Knights had also been forced to join the battle, and they were managing to keep the ghouls in check. Budibis gave up his affecting performance and hurriedly fired off another arrow, but that too was blocked by Zadilis's magic.

"You noticed too late, you dumb pig!" Zadilis cackled.

Starting midway through the battle, one of the bug undead had carried a thread-like extension of Vandal's Spirit Body over to Zadilis, providing her with magical power. No matter the number of arrows she blocked, she wasn't going to run out of MP.

Budibis switched to shooting multiple arrows, trying to turn the situation around, but his panic only reduced his accuracy. Then he started to break out Bow Proficiency skill battle techs, like Twin Shaft Shot, but those too were blocked by the wind shields. Just as he thought of using battle techs that boosted penetrating strength to cut through the wind, his Orc Knights let out screams of pain.

The cause was Skeleton Wolf, the other Rotten Beasts, and Skeleton Bird, attacking the flank of Budibis's unit with poison breath and spirit body feathers. His defenders did their job, becoming literal shields to prevent him from harm, but one of them was killed noisily in the process.

Budibis reflexively fired off a shot at the Skeleton Bear, but it was a monster of just bones, without any organs or even flesh. Shattering its spine or skull would be one thing, but a few cracked ribs weren't going to slow it down.

"Now! Take them out!" With the arrival of backup, Zadilis was assured of victory, and she gave the signal.

The ghoul mages, who had still been focused on defending and healing their protectors, now shifted to attacking, seeking to wipe out the remaining orcs. The situation had already been turning against the orcs, and an increase in the intensity of the attack was too much for them to handle. The orcs started to fall, one after the other. The final Orc Knight had its shield crushed by Bone Monkey, and then its throat torn out by Skeleton Wolf.

"Bu, buhi, buhibugyu, buhibugyu . . ."

Budibis squealed and grunted about how he couldn't believe it, how this had to be a dream. But the pain of the magic that proceeded to slam into him quickly dragged him back to reality. The cuts were shallow, but gushes of blood spurted out, snapping his fragile mind completely.

"Buhiiiiii! Bugiblio! Bubobio! Buoooo!"

Screaming for his brothers and father, Budibis turned and fled. The handsome orc face he was so proud of twisted in terror as he called for aid from the brothers he always looked down on and the father he always underestimated.

However, it wasn't the hand of a family member that reached out to him, but the scythe of death.

"You sicken me! Wind Scythe!"

Zadilis created a massive sword of wind, then used it to chop the pathetically scrambling Budibis in two.

The top half thudded down to the ground, while the bottom took a few more steps and then collapsed in a pile of organs.

Zadilis confirmed his demise, then wiped the cold sweat from her brow and gave a sigh.

"Phew. I felt you undressing me with your eyes, swine. I'm still sweating. But we're fine here now, boy."

With that comment from Zadilis, Vandal's Spirit Body stopped providing her with MP and moved on. Zadilis raised her staff and gave a shout.

"Ghouls! There are only a few enemies left! Stand fast!"

A short while earlier, the ghoul warriors, including Basdia, had quickly completed their capture of the buildings where the female ghouls were being held.

There had been orcs on watch here too, but their principle job had been more to keep the visiting orcs in line than prevent the women from escaping, and so they hadn't been especially loaded with equipment. If they were, the orcs might end up killing each other.

The orcs who had been visiting for reproductive reasons had even worse gear and were basically naked. The walls turning into Wood Golems had thrown the village into chaos, causing most of the orcs to rush outside. However, the goblins and low-ranking orcs, probably normally forced to wait their turn, now saw the opportunity, cramming the building. That was when Basdia and her warriors appeared—and the fighting was over before it even started.

The scene inside was horrible. The ghoul females had access to Brute Strength, meaning Orc Mage or Noble Orc magic had been used to partially bury the women into the stone walls to restrain them. Judging from the marks on their bodies, they had also clearly been whipped.

Some of the women hadn't received such extreme treatment, but it didn't change how terrible their situations were. Many had limbs broken in multiple places. Ghouls were far hardier than humans, meaning they could still have children for the orcs even in this condition. Hence this level of treatment.

The other women in the buildings, likely adventurers, were given better treatment, as Basdia was expecting. Although "better" wasn't a term she could realistically apply. Ghoul females were closer to monsters in terms of their values, making them more resilient to this kind of treatment.

"What to do with these women?" Basdia pondered.

The humans appeared to be completely broken. There was no light in their eyes, and they were slumped over like corpses. To Basdia, these were enemies, but it was impossible not to sympathize with them as women. She wanted to do something for them.

"Ghuuuu!"

At the call from her ally in the battle language, meaning "powerful enemy approaches," Basdia snapped back to the current situation.

"Buuoooooo!"

Basdia emerged from the building to see a Noble Orc, fangs bared and seething with anger, surrounded by Orc Knights with shields.

"Ghuuuuu!"

Her allies called for aid without hesitation. The warriors present, including Basdia, did not possess outstanding combat strength. They could defeat the Orc Knights, but the Noble Orc would give them trouble.

Even taking the support magic and gear difference into account, a group of rank 3 and 4 monsters wouldn't be able to beat ten rank 4 Orc Knights, led by a rank 6 Noble Orc. Under normal circumstances, they would be completely thrashed.

"Their leader sent this much of his strength, just to take back the women? I would have expected him to direct more of this at Vigaro," Basdia muttered, looking at the glaring Noble Orc. She and her warriors had remained here in order to prevent the Noble Orc or other minions from trying to use the captive ghoul females as hostages.

However, to put it another way, that was all that was here. Even if the orcs defeated Basdia, Vigaro, Zadilis, and Vandal would still be free to move around. Victory here wasn't going to help the orcs overall. Getting the females back might boost morale a little, but it wasn't going to change the outcome.

As a result, leaving Basdia and her warriors to their own devices and concentrating their strength on Vigaro and Zadilis made the most sense. Monsters didn't do things that made sense, of course, but a Noble Orc should have had the intellect to make better decisions.

However, applying such thinking to the young Noble Orc looking down on Basdia was to give the pigface too much credit. While aware that minions and slaves couldn't turn the situation around, the Noble Orc also had the baseless confidence that things would work out once he took to the field. His brothers had the same issue, and so they had all split up and gone their own ways, seeking to get the glory for themselves. They had no intentions of working together or helping each other out. The only thing in their heads was getting one up on their other brothers and becoming their father's favorite.

In order to achieve that, Bubobio had decided to secure the women. There weren't female Noble Orcs, or female orcs at all, so maintaining the race meant capturing women from other races. That was why he thought taking back the settlement's women would receive some praise. He wasn't thinking about winning the battle, but obtaining the most glory with as little work as possible. And upon realizing there was a tough-looking female among the enemies, with plenty of meat on her—that being Basdia—his beastly desires for her to bear his child reared up.

He clearly wasn't operating on common sense.

"Buoooooh!" Bubobio gave the order to capture the female alive, pointing at Basdia with the tip of his massive sword.

The Orc Knights raised their shields and hunched over.

"Ghuuuu! (They're about to charge!)" one ghoul shouted.

"Gaarrrl! (Buy us some time!)" Basdia replied.

They needed to hold out until backup arrived. Basdia and the ghouls prepared to take their lumps, with the ten Orc Knights all about to trigger Shield Bash . . . and then the ground started to move.

"Raaaaaaaaaaaaah!"

The ground turned into dozens of earth golems and rose up in front of the Orc Knights. Comprised of nothing but crumbly earth, the golems should not have been able to withstand a single Shield Bash from any of the hefty orcs. They should have crumbled away in an instant. But instead—

"Bugiaaaah?!"

Before the Orc Knights could smash into the earth golems, they tripped on the holes created in the floor and tumbled down into it. The earth golems had been created from the ground, which left behind earth golem–sized holes. Once the Orc Knights tumbled in, the freshly risen Earth Golems proceeded to fall back in on top of them, burying them alive.

Basdia, the other ghouls, and Bubobio were all frozen in place, stunned by this rapid and unexpected chain of events. Neither side spoke for a moment.

"That was even more effective than I expected. I think I'll call it . . . the golem instant pit trap technique!" Vandal called, pulling up in Sam.

What terrifying power you wield, young master. I am impressed, Sam replied, his wheels clattering as they spun.

"Van? That was you?" Basdia finally managed.

"Yes, all me," the toddler said. "The Noble Orc is still alive and kicking, so let's not drop our guard yet."

"S-sure thing."

"The leader of these orcs is still alive too. Hurry up and take care of this."

"I understand—hold on! I'm doing the defeating here?!" she exclaimed.

"Yes. It will be good experience for you," Vandal replied, casually asking her to do nothing less than defeat Bubobio. "It'll be fine. I've got your back."

"I don't think that's going to help me defeat a Noble Orc!"

"If you think something is impossible, then it will be," Vandal quipped. "To quote a shitty doctor who only believed in results."

"So am I meant to follow his advice or not?!"

"No, he was a real rotten-brained asshole," Vandal said. If that doctor was going to treat Vandal like little more than a lab rat, the responsibility for his failures should have fallen on his own shoulders—but he was just a whiner, always blaming Vandal if something went wrong. The only time Vandal had ever liked the guy was when he was screaming at the moment of his death. He had been blond too, Vandal recalled, as he looked at Bubobio.

"It'll be fine," Vandal said. "So long as I protect you, you're safe. Here he comes!"

Basdia gave a start and raised her axe. She faced down Bubobio, who was shaking with anger at being ignored.

"Gubooooooh!"

The two of them were chattering away, completely oblivious to him! He roared and raised his massive sword in anger just as the earth where the Orc Knights were buried started to writhe and churn.

Vandal hadn't been able to dig deep enough to finish them off, and so he had been expecting them to climb back out at some point. He kept his cool.

"Rita, Saria, everyone else. Finish off the buried ones," Vandal commanded. "Basdia and I will handle the Noble Orc."

"If that's how it's gonna be!" Basdia wasn't sure this was a good idea, but she stepped forward regardless.

Behind her, the screams of the Orc Knights rang out as a glaive, a halberd, or claws ended their lives just as they struggled back up to the surface.

Bubobio rushed at Basdia with a roar, like a wall charging at her. The orc swung his massive axe downward too fast for her eyes to follow, arching straight toward her head.

Dodge right. Basdia followed her instincts and avoided the swift, killer attack.

Bubobio roared with rage at his attack whiffing. He dragged the blade back to unleash a thrust forward.

Half step left. Basdia dodged that too, before she even realized it.

"Bu—bu! Buooh! Bugogoh!" snarled Bubobio. Perhaps having both attacks dodged so easily made him panic a little, and he shifted to a series of rapid attacks. There was the horizontal Flicker Slash, the diagonal Flowing Slice, the Three Tier Thrust targeting the head, body, and belly, and then the Three Tier Slice targeting the neck, belly, and legs. They were all especially nasty battle techs, any one of them likely to cause crippling damage even to Basdia's honed body beneath her superior armor.

But Basdia dodged them all.

Bubobio's face was painted with an ugly depiction of surprise, wondering how such a thing could possibly be. There was no way, in his understanding, that a female ghoul could move fast enough to avoid his invincible sword strokes. He passed through rage and entered the realm of fear.

Basdia was just as surprised—she couldn't believe she was dodging them. Actually fighting the orc, she realized it didn't possess a fighting technique that was particularly superior to her own. On that score they were evenly matched, almost. But their basic physical strength was worlds apart. She might have gotten lucky and avoided one or two of these, but a succession of such strikes should have chopped her to pieces by now. But for some reason, Basdia knew what she needed to do in order to avoid that fate.

She felt she needed to move right, and when she quickly did so, the sword slashed down through where she had just been standing. She felt she needed to drop back, and when she rushed to do so, the tip of the sword slashed across where she stood instants before. It was like she could see the future—like she had obtained the skill Future Foresight. She just knew exactly what she had to do in order to avoid death.

Ah! This is coming from Van's support!

Chilly, soft hands were supporting her. It was those hands that told her how to avoid death.

Vandal used Spirit Bodification on his arms and merged them with Basdia's back. Through those arms, Vandal's constantly active Detect Danger: Death also applied to Basdia. Detect Danger: Death foresaw coming death, so there was no way it could ignore the deadly swings of Bubobio's sword. If she had been fighting a kobolt, seeking to win by a series of lighter attacks, or if the Noble Orc had calmed down a little and refined his technique, Detect Danger: Death would not have been activated so easily, and things might not have been this one-sided. But Bubobio was angry, panicked, and scared, completely losing his cool. So he continued to unleash a string of the most powerful attacks he could muster.

In reality, the three Noble Orc brothers were pretty pathetic representatives of their race. It wasn't so much what they had been born with as the environment into which they had been born, and Bugogan's complete failure to raise them correctly.

They had been born in these demon barrens after Bugogan fled here, meaning since the moment of their birth, they had been surrounded by nothing but lower orcs, plus goblin and kobolt slaves. Their natural raw strength had always been enough to handle most issues they faced, and even if they did encounter a skilled enemy, simply swinging their weapons hard enough and fast enough had always been enough.

This meant they rarely trained, and as they were only fighting inferior opponents, their levels never increased either. All of their combat skills were stuck at level 3, and they hardly knew any magic at all, due to it being difficult and time-consuming to learn. The only rivals they really had to compete with were their own brothers, who had similar abilities to each other. Rather than push each other to improve, they settled for trying to find easy ways to make the others look bad.

If this place had been the harsh environment of the massive demon barren in the south of the continent, with plenty of other Noble Orcs and monsters equal in strength to them, Bubobio and his brothers wouldn't have been able to slack off and squander their talents so easily.

Bugogan's attitude also played a part, of course. He believed that a child who grew up without guidance from a parent was strong, while a child who needed constant attention was weak. If Bugogan cast that aside and trained his children himself, they might have achieved powerful combat and magical abilities. But he had ended up with three dumb sons who had only ever experienced victory against soft, easy opponents.

That hadn't been a problem until now, because soft and easy was all they had ever needed to beat. But Basdia and the ghouls had studied and trained far harder than the orcs, honing their skills. The ghouls had gear from Vandal and Talea that outstripped equipment used by many adventurers. Add in the magical support and effects of Enhance Brethren and the ghouls could not only fill in the rank gap, but completely overtake it.

Despite all of that, it should have been difficult for Basdia to defeat Bubobio unscathed. With Vandal's support, however, she certainly wasn't going to die. And if one side couldn't possibly die in a one-on-one fight, then that side's victory was assured.

Bubobio grunted and gasped as he ran out of steam, his movements slowing down and his battle techs grinding to a halt. Using battle techs cost MP, but in this case, his muscles were also on the verge of giving out.

"Cleave!"

"Bugiiiiii!"

Basdia switched to the attack, and Bubobio squealed as her axe lopped off one of his arms.

She continued, showing no mercy as she unleashed a sequence of battle techs. Steel Flash, Swift Response, then Flicker Flash.

Bubobio gave up and turned to flee—which was when Basdia used the Thrown Projectile Proficiency battle tech Pierce to launch her axe into the back of the orc's skull. His corpse collapsed face-first onto the ground.

"I did it! I defeated him, Van! I took down a Noble Orc!" Basdia exclaimed, high on the surge of experience from defeating such a powerful foe. She dashed over to Sam and snatched Vandal up from the wagon, swinging him around.

"You did. I saw it. You defeated him, so please put me down," Vandal said. He was happy that she was happy, but having his vision rocking about like a ship in a storm wasn't exactly comfortable. And the other ghouls were too busy celebrating to stop Basdia.

At least she had gained the experience from the encounter, just as Vandal had planned. Due to the curse, Vandal couldn't earn experience for himself. Even if he did earn it vicariously, at the moment he was already level 100, so it would just go to waste. That was why he wanted Basdia to get the kill, as she could make better use of the experience.

"Now we just need to deal with their father—" Vandal started, and then a terrible roar cut him off, ringing out from the largest of the houses in the settlement.

"BUGAAAAAAAAAAH!"

The roar caused the walls of the building to explode, but was so loud that it even drowned out the noise of the destruction.

From the wreckage emerged a massive Noble Orc, more than ten feet tall. He was dressed in extravagant armor and had a massive demon sword that was itself over six feet long.

Vandal and Basdia could see the orc clearly from where they were standing. Its raw strength erased all chatter and drained away the morale of their forces. That was inevitable. This was a real Noble Orc: a monster on equal footing with a dragon.

Having escaped from Basdia's hands, Vandal used his Detect Danger: Death skill to analyze the threat posed by this raging Noble Orc, Bugogan. He had to try and work out how they could win.

If he carried on from their previous battle, fighting in co-operation with Basdia . . . whatever he did, or didn't do, Basdia would die.

If they waited for Zadilis, and then fought mainly using magic . . . whatever he did, or didn't do, multiple frontline and backline ghouls, including Zadilis, would die.

If they fought centered around Vigaro, based in close combat . . . whatever he did, or didn't do, and whether they got lucky or unlucky, Vigaro would die. If Zadilis, Vigaro, and Basdia all took the lead together, and then Sam, Vandal, and everyone else backed them up . . . then they could win. But no matter how lucky they got, some of them were going to die.

But if Vandal fought Bugogan alone, with support from everyone else . . . his chances of dying were over fifty percent, but everyone else survived more than ninety percent of the time.

"Watch my back, please," Vandal said.

Before anyone even had the time to react to his comment, Vandal activated the non-attribute magic Flight. He rose up into the air and flew off toward Bugogan as fast as a bullet.

Bugogan had finished his preparations for battle, but he had remained seated on his throne until he heard the final screams of his stupid, pathetic sons.

He was their king. The king didn't fight on the field of battle. That duty fell to his sons with their lust for advancement, his other minions, and his slaves.

Thus, Bugogan had remained seated on his throne, berating his pathetic underlings and telling his son to get out there and fight for him. He was still sitting in his throne room when he realized all the minions and slaves were gone, and his sons had all been killed.

That was when Bugogan's anger boiled over.

"BUGAAAAAAAAAAAH!"

He snatched up his demon sword and rose from the throne. The walls of his own abode had received more attention than general orc homes, but they were still pretty crude. He smashed through them without issue.

Fragments of wood scattered everywhere, and he gave another roar. But his rage burned on.

How much did he suffer to breed this many orcs? His sons were dumb and stupid and pathetic, but it had been a struggle to breed them too. Getting that many slaves, women, weapons, armor, all of it together had been so difficult—and in a single night, it was all reduced to nothing. He couldn't stand it.

He cursed the ghouls. He would kill all the men, capture all the women, and make as many new orcs as he had lost!

As he raged on, he saw something flying in toward him at incredible speed.

He considered it as nothing more than part of the scenery, until it stopped about thirty feet in front of him. Once he confirmed what it was, he was so puzzled that he forgot his anger.

It looked like a human child, with unruly white hair, white skin, one bloodred eye, and one purple eye. For a moment he thought maybe it was an albino ghoul child, but he got a glimpse of its ears and saw they were pointed. That suggested elf blood was in the mix.

But more than the physical appearance, Bugogan was more perplexed by the fact he didn't feel anything coming from the child.

No presence, no sound, no smells, no intent to kill, no hostility, no fear, nothing.

If someone told him this was a hallucination, he would have believed it. If he closed his eyes, the baby would seem to vanish altogether. It stayed floating in the air, then spread its arms as though attempting to block his path. Black magical power then swelled up around it.

Bugogan finally worked it out. This was his enemy.

Bugogan, the Noble Orc. Vandal, the Ghoul King. The start of the battle between these titans was as witless as it got.

Vandal wreathed himself in death attribute magic and activated Anti-Attack Barrier and Magic Sucking Barrier. Meanwhile, Bugogan just stood and watched.

Immediately after Vandal activated his barriers, Bugogan grunted out a short spell. It caused a spear of earth to suddenly erupt up from below Vandal. For a moment it looked like he was going to get skewered in the feet, but the moment it touched his Anti-Attack Barrier, it crumbled back into earth.

The combination of the Anti-Attack Barrier and Magic Sucking Barrier sapped the strength from all forms of exterior attack. It took electrical energy from lightning, heat energy from fire, and magical power from magic. It easily nullified Bugogan's spell.

"Bubu, bugah!" Bugogan grunted, realizing the barriers were to blame.

Deciding that close combat was more likely to work than magic, Bugogan raised his demon sword. In the next instant, and with a fierce battle cry, the orc closed in with Vandal. At an impossibly fast speed, rocketing down from Bugogan's ten-foot-tall and wide frame, the demon sword swung down at Vandal.

The attack looked ready to cleave through rock like paper, but the Anti-Attack Barrier blocked it. It didn't leave so much as a scratch on Vandal. Bugogan had read the situation completely wrong: the Anti-Attack Barrier absorbed not just magical power but also the kinetic energy from physical attacks.

Kinetic energy was the force required to move something.

Moving dumbbells that weighed ten kilograms required ten kilograms of energy. The Anti-Attack Barrier could absorb that energy, meaning Bugogan's demon sword couldn't reach Vandal inside the barrier.

Bugogan's face twisted. Attacking this tiny creature felt strange, like it was surrounded by a soft wall.

Vandal, meanwhile, was looking at Bugogan from behind the sword that had stopped in front of his face. His expression didn't change, but he had a thought.

Oh crap. I'm gonna die.

It looked like Vandal was protected by an impenetrable steel wall, but that wall was not going to last forever. *Blocking that last attack, which wasn't even a battle tech, cost me 5,000 MP*, Vandal thought. Vandal had been burning through his MP since the battle started, so he already had less than half left. He still had a big chunk, but it could take tens of thousands, if not millions, of MP to block a single battle tech from Bugogan. Of course, using battle techs also cost MP, so Bugogan wouldn't be able to unleash them endlessly either. But the orc had already proven he could use magic, which suggested a bigger MP pool than his sons. He surely had a lot of stamina too. When Vandal's MP ran out, and the barriers came down, Vandal would have no escape.

Because I'm weak.

If someone asked Vandal if he was strong, he would reply that no, he was weak. He had death attribute magic, which only he could use. He had more than one hundred million MP. As a dhampir, he was stronger than a grown man even at just two years old. But he was weak, all the same. If all the living creatures on Ramda were divided up into those who were weak and those who were strong, Vandal would be on the weak side, without question.

For a start, death attribute magic was much more restrictive than other types of magic and could only do limited things. It had almost no spells that caused direct damage. Nothing like Fire Lance, or Earth Axe, or Spatial Stab. It was great for defense, as he was currently proving, but he couldn't go on the attack either. Eventually he was going to lose.

It didn't matter if he had one hundred million MP, two hundred, or a billion. When his vitality ran out, he was dead.

He might have physical abilities in excess of a regular human male, but that was nothing compared to the dragon-level monster in front of him.

So he was weak. He didn't have unassailable strength that he could fall back on. And yet he couldn't just give up and die.

"Rise!"

First, he turned the ground at Bugogan's feet into golems in an attempt to bring him down. If he could stop the big orc from moving around, Basdia and the others could attack from long range and finish him off.

But Bugogan easily stamped out the Earth Golems that tried to cling to him. He used the Brawling Proficiency battle tech Kicker, allowing him to crush multiple golems with a single strike. Vandal had hoped it might at least buy him some time. But it wasn't enough—he'd have to burn tens of thousands of MP for just a few seconds of distraction.

Next, Vandal unleashed the non-attribute spell MP Shot. This was a simple attack that created a ball of magical power and smashed it into the target. As it was non-attribute, it could be expected to cause some damage to any enemy.

He poured in around 10,000 MP, firing off a succession of MP Shots about the same size as his own body, targeting different areas. He finished the sequence with a massive MP Shot, adding 100,000 MP into it.

If they hit their target, they should have sent even Bugogan flying to the edges of his own settlement.

But the orc decided to use his sword to block them.

"Buooooooooooooh!" Bugogan roared, slashing the air at tremendous speeds and sending all the MP Shots flying away. He was using a battle tech that increased his reaction speed—not Swift Response, but the promoted skill Super Swift Response—plus the defensive battle tech Shot Sweeper, to knock the shots away with his sword, enhancing the blade with further magical power.

Vandal was actually impressed. A highly skilled swordsman would have difficulty pulling that move off. Vandal hadn't been expecting the father of that reject Bubobio to be quite so powerful.

Vandal's Magic Control skill was still comparatively low when compared to the MP he had poured into the deflected MP Shot. This meant that his MP dissipated almost immediately instead of the errant missiles wreaking havoc on their surroundings. Vandal's Detect Life observed an immobile life form inside the house Bugogan had emerged from, which Vandal had taken into consideration when deciding the arc of his shots.

After knocking all the MP Shots aside, Bugogan swung his sword down with a shout, activating the battle tech Cross Slash. The Anti-Attack Barrier made an odd noise—it was unable to instantly absorb the sword's destructive force, and the blade buried itself halfway into the barrier.

I can't lose my cool.

Bugogan's eyes were bulging at getting blocked again—he had probably been hoping to end it with that attack—while Vandal poured more MP into the Anti-Attack Barrier, shoring it up against further assault. That Cross Slash would have quartered and killed your average knight or adventurer. Not to mention that Cross Slash was a lower-level battle tech than the Super Swift Response attack that Bugogan had already used. It suggested Bugogan had even more powerful battle techs just waiting to be used.

If he went full speed right away, I might have been dead already, Vandal thought.

The Anti-Attack Barrier protected him from almost all attacks, but there were ways to break it. Commonly seen when the hero of some tale needed to overcome the antagonist's attack barrier, one idea was to focus more energy than the barrier could absorb on a single point of it and defeat the caster with one blow. Essentially, strongarm it. Vandal had loved this kind of approach in fiction when he was back on Earth, but it was different when he was potentially on the receiving end. Bugogan surely had what it took to pull something like that off.

Vandal had no intention of falling to the ambitions of a Noble Orc, however. He still needed to avenge and revive his mother. That meant he needed to come up with a way to kill this swine. That led him to place a Lemure behind Bugogan. The familiar unleashed its own brand of chilling terror, and a moment later, Vandal unleashed more MP Shots.

The Lemures popped, causing a pulse of intense hostility directly behind Bugogan.

"Bugii?!" Bugogan whipped around, unable to ignore such

a sensation even with one enemy directly in front of him. The more sensitive he was to such threats—the better the warrior— the bigger the unconscious reaction. Vandal's plan was to then Swiss-cheese him with MP Shots. Simple, effective, what could go wrong—

Bugogan applied Super Swift Response again, boosting his reaction speed, making full use of his flexible, powerful upper body to launch the battle tech Blade Dance. This variable, multi-hitting attack allowed him to strike at both the Lemures behind him and the MP Shots closing in from the front.

"BUGAAAAAAH!"

The demon sword glittered in the moonlight as it thrashed around, flashing through the black orbs of death and scattering them in every direction. You could even call it beautiful. To Vandal, it looked like the twinkling of a star.

Then he had a premonition of death. He thickened the Anti-Attack Barrier once more.

With a growl, Bugogan jabbed the tip of his sword at Vandal, using the skill Piercing Thrust. The cold steel stopped a few millimeters away from Vandal. He would never have been able to react quickly enough without Detect Danger: Death. He had underestimated Bugogan's combat strength, to say the orc had recovered from the terror of the Lemures and all the MP Shots before launching his own attack.

What do I have left that I could kill him with? Maybe scatter disease in the air using Generate Sickness? But no, it would take too long for the orc to fall sick. Vandal would run out of MP first. But maybe he could use Virulent Poison, somehow. He wasn't sure how, while fighting such a powerful enemy. Things had worked out when dealing with the Kobolt King Gyahn, but this was a very different story.

Confusing him with golems, then? That seemed worth a try. Bugogan was preparing to attack again, and so before he had a chance, Vandal used Flight to pull back and muttered, "Rise!"

The earth groaned and screeched as Earth Golems rose up behind Bugogan and Wood Golems emerged from the scattered rubble. Vandal even resurrected the bodies of goblins and kobolts as zombies. At the same time, he tried to destabilize Bugogan by turning the ground at his feet into more Earth Golems as he unleashed more MP Shots and Lemures.

"Bugah!" Bugogan roared, closing in on Vandal. He used Blade Dance to shred apart the MP Shots and golems, and activated Kicker to smash the ones by his feet. He was using Kicker with every step he took, making sure the ground didn't give out beneath him, but with every step, the ground shook and shuddered.

It was starting to feel like whoever ran out of stamina or MP first would lose the battle—and then Vandal heard his allies' shouts.

"Attack!"

Young master!

The shouts were accompanied by arrows, spears, poison breath, Spirit Body feathers, bolts of fire and stone, and clumps of ice and wind, all seeking to eradicate Bugogan completely.

Zadilis and the others had turned up.

Bellowing madly, Bugogan used his peerless armor, powerful muscles, and demon sword to repel the supporting storm of attacks from Vandal's allies. The blade could shred even the poison breath and magic spells apart. Their target wasn't completely unharmed, but didn't suffer more than a few scratches.

This is bad. How do I settle this? His allies had now gathered, and Vandal still had no idea how to land a finishing blow.

Bugogan seemed fixated on killing Vandal, but also unlikely to give chase if Vandal decided to run. The worst thing that could happen was Bugogan changing targets. Anyone else he targeted was not going to get out alive.

I can't let them die. He might have been able to keep them around as spirits, as he was doing with Dalshia. He might be able to restore Sam and the other undead, so long as their souls were intact. *But what if that sword has the ability to injure Spirit Bodies?* No, he couldn't have that. Unacceptable. Not on his watch. He had to kill this pig before something like that happened.

But how? How can I break through the powerful guard of this creature and cause fatal damage?

Vandal thought so hard smoke was coming out of his ears, and then it suddenly hit him. A method that Bugogan wouldn't be able to avoid or defend against.

It was so simple. Nothing special.

Vandal had to suffer a fatal wound. That was all.

In the next moment, Bugogan's demon sword shredded the Anti-Attack Barrier in the very spot that Vandal had intentionally weakened it, and the blade tore into his body—

Vandal hadn't realized it, with Bugogan's string of raging attacks, but the orc was actually losing ground. In fact, from the orc's perspective, he was the one on the ropes.

This unknown enemy was right in front of him but didn't have any presence. The small creature was unleashing wave after wave of deadly attacks, but didn't have the slightest hint of hostility.

The power held by the MP Shots Vandal so casually tossed out would normally take everything a skilled magician had to produce. Vandal's lack of MP control reduced their overall power, but they were still strong enough to shatter Bugogan's bones and organs if he took one head-on. Each time he deflected one with his sword, he felt a brutal impact, which was placing a rapidly accumulating burden on his wrists. He had no idea how much longer he could even hold his sword.

Then there were the unknown, invisible enemies that unleashed powerful waves of hostility, the earth and rubble that suddenly came to life, and corpses turning into zombies. He tried to respond with magic, but anything that involved releasing MP beyond his own body simply didn't work, blocked by the black mist surrounding the creature. Forced to rely on his MP and muscles in the form of battle techs, Bugogan gathered all of the physical and mental fortitude he had left—and then enemy reinforcements arrived.

The situation seemed hopeless. He wanted to shout, to rail against how unfair it was. He couldn't hope to target any enemies other than Vandal or try and run away. If he took his eyes off his main enemy, how would he block those MP Shots? It took all of his focus to stay aware of this enemy who could conceal his presence so completely. If Bugogan turned his back, he would be finished, punched through by an MP Shot and killed.

The thing that scared Bugogan the most, however, was Vandal's expressionless face. Those eyes, fixed right on him. No matter what happened, his face betrayed no emotion.

No exhaustion, fear, panic. No anything.

Bugogan interpreted this expression as the enemy having strength to spare. That this was a foe who could keep on going, for hours, for days if necessary. If Bugogan couldn't find a way to respond, his strength was going to give out, and he was going to die.

Defeat and death lay before the Noble Orc.

"Bugaaaaah!"

Believing that he had been cornered, Bugogan could only come up with one strategy: kill Vandal, and then use his remaining strength to scatter the ghouls and make a run for it.

That was when one of his attacks finally found its target. It wasn't deep enough to cleave his enemy in two, but from the response he felt down the blade, he was sure it had reached body and organs. Bugogan's mouth lifted in a smile.

"Van!"

"Boy!"

As the ghouls shrieked, Bugogan became convinced of his victory. He had used a lot of his strength and MP, but still had a quarter left. More than enough to scatter this rabble. He would have preferred to slaughter them all, but that would come later. So long as he survived, he could build his nation again. Gather minions and slaves, have more sons, and form the ultimate orc kingdom.

He licked at the unexpectedly warm blood that had splattered onto his face . . . and then Bugogan dropped to his knees.

It worked. The big blood splash really helped.

Vandal had dropped to the ground, unable to breathe with the sword cutting into his lungs, so he watched Bugogan go down in silence.

In the moment the sword hit him, he had used Spirit Bodification on his heart and spine and moved them out behind him, meaning his limbs still worked. He had lost a lot of blood, which was rough, but he wasn't going to die, unless he suffocated.

Now he was using tens of thousands of MP on the non-attribute magic Enhanced Healing, prioritizing the repair of his lungs. It was lucky that Bugogan's sword was so sharp. The cut was clean and easy to repair, but he still coughed and spat up blood.

"Boy, don't move! Let me tend to you!" Zadilis said.

"Pig! You pay for killing Vandal!" Vigaro roared.

Wait, wait. I was just spitting up blood that entered my throat, Vandal thought. *I'll be able to breathe again shortly. I'm not dead yet, Vigaro.*

Young master, we are the only ones who can hear your thoughts like that, Sam said.

I know that.

"Sam, what is Van saying?!" Basdia asked.

It is okay, everyone. The young master will soon be healed, Sam reported.

The plan Vandal had used was to suffer an injury not severe enough to kill him—that he could heal on his own—and then turn the blood spilling from it into Virulent Poison to land on Bugogan.

The orc had no idea that the blood splatter was poison, taking the highly toxic blood to his face and even licking some up. His arms and legs became paralyzed, his mind fogged over, his vision clouded, and then his head spasmed. The effects of the ultra-potent poison made Bugogan unable to even hold up his sword. First unable to rise from his knees, the Noble Orc then dropped onto his face.

First, finish off the Noble Orc. Be careful not to touch the young master's blood—

"Gaaah!" Vigaro immediately shouted, having touched some of the blood.

"Vigaro!"

Poison doesn't work on us. One of us should have handled that. Oh, very well. Sam moved over to the collapsed Bugogan and wheeled over his neck with a nasty popping noise.

That was the end of the ambitions of the Noble Orc: a brutal, empty ending, with zero honor.

And so the clash between the Ghoul King and Noble Orc came to an end, with the majority of the drama coming from each side completely overestimating the other.

It was over, but there was still plenty to do.

"Someone said that it's only after the war ends that the real work begins," Vandal muttered. The cleanup operation.

The first thing to do, of course, was use Detoxify to remove the poison from Vigaro. The ghouls with comparatively more strength left were put on watch to keep away any other monsters attracted by the smell of blood. The ghoul females started caring for the captive ghouls. Others searched the remaining buildings for any remaining enemies and prepared somewhere for their allies to start getting some rest.

There was a dizzying amount to do.

Vandal had sent Skeleton Bird to report to the Ghoul Grotto. Vandal had less than twenty percent of his stamina and MP left, but he couldn't take a break yet.

"It's mellow and rich, but with a lingering aftertaste," Vandal said aloud. Luckily, there was plenty of fresh food lying around. He was draining the orcs while also using their blood to recover his strength and MP—that was the only reason he could keep going.

Tomorrow he was going to have to turn the tumbled Entwood fence back into golems and erect the wall again. And that would be only the beginning of the challenges ahead.

"Boy. I know you're busy, so we can do this later, but I need to talk to you," Zadilis said.

"And I with you," Vandal replied.

I think Lady Dalshia will want some words with you too, young master, Sam commented. *She is not going to be happy about how you concluded your encounter.*

". . . Yeah," Vandal finally replied. His plan of poisoning his opponent by allowing damage to his flesh, organs, and bones might have worked out, but it had clearly upset Zadilis and the others. *I'd rather avoid a chewing-out, if it can be helped,* Vandal pondered. Vigaro's take on the events had been more favorable: he had praised Vandal's bravery and called him a real man. That was something.

"Vandal. I can lecture you tomorrow," Zadilis said. "For today, we need to discuss what to do with the human women."

"We can hardly tell them to keep quiet and then let them go in the closest town . . . can we?" Vandal asked, maybe a little too hopefully.

"Hmmm. Even if there was a town nearby, I fear they would just slump down in place and die on the spot."

"Yeah, good point."

Defeating the evil monsters didn't mean everyone got a happy ending.

Name: Bugogan
Rank: 7
Race: Noble Orc Leader
Level: 100
——**Passive Skills**
[Brute Strength: Level 4] [Energy Boost: Level 3] [Lower Race Rule: Level 3]
——**Active Skills**
[Sword Proficiency: Level 6] [Brawling Proficiency: Level 4] [Earth Attribute Magic: Level 4] [Fire Attribute Magic: Level 3] [Non-Attribute Magic: Level 2] [Magic Control: Level 3]

The Death Mage

CHAPTER FOUR

THE ENEMY OF MY ENEMY
IS MY NEW ENEMY

The woman lay on the bed, staring at the ceiling like a corpse.

It should be over now?

It wasn't "like" a corpse, but actually was one. The woman was one of the Living Dead, created by forcing vitality back into a fresh corpse, using life attribute magic to restore basic functions like a pulse and breathing. This particular Living Dead was the familiar of the adventurer known as "The Depraved," one Luchiriano. He had sent it in to investigate the movements of the Noble Orcs, taking advantage of their biology and sexual proclivities.

The Living Dead had dull senses, and its master had been using them—in particular the hearing—to follow the clashes of swords and screams that had rung out until a short while previously. Now he couldn't hear them at all.

The ghouls put up more of a fight than I expected, Luchiriano thought. *We might not need a large force after all.*

His own master, Viscount Valchez, had been left with no choice but to beg the Milg Shield Kingdom Marshal Count Palpapekk for a loan of more forces because this orc settlement had reached almost unheard-of numbers. If the battle with the ghouls had reduced that to a third, however, ten parties of grade C adventurers would be enough to handle the remaining problem.

The report that Bugogan's sons and most of the other commander classes, such as the Orc Generals and Orc Mages, had all been taken out had been delivered with such urgency to Bugogan that even the Living Dead's muffled hearing detected it clearly. That meant the only threat to grade C adventurers would be Bugogan himself, and although Bugogan was a threat, he was still rank 7. Sure, that was the same rank as an Earth Dragon, but it wasn't anything a bunch of grade C adventurers couldn't handle if they all worked together.

Hiring grade C adventurers wasn't cheap, but it was much cheaper than putting together a force of hundreds. And unlike soldiers or knights, these were hires for one job, meaning it was no loss to Valchez if some of them paid the ultimate price along the way.

Luchiriano was thinking all of these matters over when someone entered the house that its enraged owner had seen fit to destroy. Sensing their presence, he stopped thinking about anything. The footsteps were too quiet to be Bugogan returning in victory, and he sensed multiple entities. He wondered if some goblins were using the chaos of the battle to move around more freely.

"There. Look human," said a voice.

"Is it alive?" asked another.

But the figures that appeared were lion-headed male ghouls. Luchiriano's eyes opened in surprise.

The ghouls defeated that Noble Orc?! Luchiriano had heard that higher ranks of ghouls, such as Ghoul Tyrants or Ghoul Elder Mages, were not to be found in this jungle. Defeating the Noble Orc was beyond anything Luchiriano had been expecting.

And not just Luchiriano. No one would have expected a horde of more than 400 monsters, led by a Noble Orc, to get wiped out by in-fighting within a demon barren.

No matter how hard it was to accept, however, the ghouls weren't going anywhere.

"It just moved. It alive."

"Okay. Take to other humans."

"Wait a moment," came a third voice, and a female ghoul joined the two males. "At least cover her before carrying her around."

The female then used a fur from the bed to cover the exposed Living Dead, which had been left there midway through the act with Bugogan.

Luchiriano's stomach churned at this seeming kindness. *If the ghouls have won, there's no hope of saving the captured women now*, he thought. All adventurers knew that ghouls ate human flesh. They were probably going to throw a celebratory banquet, feasting on the women whom the orcs had been holding. Either that, or hold their unholy ritual performed to turn the humans into ghouls.

In either case, there was no saving them. *Considering the life awaiting them after being rescued, they would probably be happier dying now anyway*, Luchiriano pondered. They were victims, defiled by the orcs, and Luchiriano knew that it was unlikely for them to be happy again, even if they were saved.

Once more than a month had passed since their capture, the overbearing sexual drives and terrible handling of their orc captors would have terribly damaged them not only physically but also mentally, making it almost impossible for them to recover. They would be unable to return to a life as adventurers from that state, and even if they wanted to, the orcs had taken all their gear. The women were all grade D or lower, meaning even if they had some money held with the guild, it wouldn't be enough to replace everything they had lost.

But retiring from the adventurer life was no better a choice. They would be treated as filth if knowledge of what the orcs had done got out. No one would seriously consider marriage and finding any kind of regular work would be hard.

If they were regular village girls, they could expect some aid from the government. Viscount Valchez was, from Luchiriano's perspective, a decent noble. While he wouldn't take care of the victims for life, a year or two of support probably wasn't asking too much. But these women had been adventurers. In principle, adventurers had to take responsibility for anything and everything that happened to them on the job. They couldn't expect government support. They might get living expenses for one month. The princess being saved from her captivity by a hero and living happily ever after was something that only happened in stories.

All of this was better than the way they would've been treated in the past, of course, which might have included getting executed as a "witch who lent her womb to a monster" or simply being treated as booty by the adventurers who slayed their captors and sold off as slaves.

As Luchiriano considered the merciless world, the ghouls started to carry his Living Dead away. He was sure the body was about to be eaten, but as the Living Dead didn't feel any pain, at least he wasn't going to have to experience that. He therefore had decided to gather as much information as he could before the Living Dead was destroyed.

I only see orc, kobolt, and goblin corpses lying around. I don't see any ghouls' bodies.

Luchiriano hadn't seen the actual battle, so he had no idea what went on outside. He moved the eyeballs of the Living Dead around to take in the vicinity—and the information he collected made him feel pretty sick. Or at least, that was how it was going to make his employers, Viscount Valchez and Marshal Palpapekk, feel. The ghouls didn't seem to have taken much damage, and there were more than one hundred of them. For some reason, they were also pretty well equipped, with some of them even carrying what looked like magic items.

"This is all thanks to our king! The ultimate king, defeating a Noble Orc one-on-one!"

"Hurray for the Ghoul King! Hurray for Vandal!"

Luchiriano heard shouts from the victorious ghouls. It sounded like a Ghoul King had appeared, blessed with superior command and physical strength, some way to acquire powerful weapons, and strong enough to defeat a rank 7 monster in a one-on-one battle.

Once this Living Dead is destroyed, I'm not accepting any extension to this job! No matter how they beg! Luchiriano wanted nothing to do with fighting more than one hundred ghouls, led by a king. It didn't matter how much money they were willing to pay. He wouldn't be able to spend it if he wasn't alive.

For some reason, the walls around the settlement had also come down, replaced by logs all scattered around. He wondered if that was also the work of the Ghoul King.

I also heard that "king" was only used as a title when one of them brought multiple settlements together, Luchiriano thought. Then his Living Dead was dropped down onto the floor in one of the comparatively intact houses.

"Wait here. Vandal come soon."

The ghouls that had carried in the Living Dead departed. They didn't leave anyone on watch, so they didn't seem to consider him a threat.

They don't see me as an enemy but as food, Luchiriano reasoned. Numerous women surrounded his Living Dead. All of them were human, with dead-looking eyes and marks on their hands, feet, and faces. Some of them just groaned, while others begged quietly to be killed.

Even Luchiriano, known as the Depraved, wanted to cover his ears and shut out these terrible sounds. They were clearly the adventurers who had been captured by the orcs. As adventurers, they should have been tougher both mentally and physically than regular women, but the orcs had completely broken them. Luchiriano didn't want to see these women eaten alive. If possible, he wished he could have killed them himself.

Luchiriano gave a start of surprise.

There was a child standing there, staring at him. Luchiriano had no idea when the child had appeared. The child had one red and one violet eye, both staring right at Luchiriano. He looked young, only around three years old. Luchiriano had no idea why he was in such a place.

Is this a dhampir? Luchiriano thought. *Why is there a dhampir child here? Where are his parents? There were no subordinate vampires under the Noble Orc. Is this vampire working with the ghouls?* All sorts of questions filled Luchiriano's mind, but the next words from the dhampir child's mouth erased them all.

"What are you doing in there?" the child asked. "That's someone else's body."

He knows this is a Living Dead?! Impossible! Almost no one can see through this technique! Luchiriano was stunned.

The dhampir closed in. "At your side there, the spirit of that woman is possessing her own body. She's telling you to give it back and stop defiling her."

He can see spirits? Is he some kind of medium? Luchiriano was a skilled life attribute mage, but he had never had a Medium job and so he couldn't see spirits himself. He hadn't realized that the spirit of the corpse they had used to make the Living Dead was tagging along the whole time.

There was no talking his way out of this one. But Luchiriano also wasn't overly flustered by this development. After all, he was only sharing his senses with the Living Dead. He wasn't actually there. He could return his consciousness at any time, leaving the demon barrens behind. Whatever the dhampir did to the Living Dead he left behind, he wouldn't feel any of it.

"Please don't run away." The dhampir proceeded to stick his hand into the body of the Living Dead.

That cold hand grabbed Luchiriano's consciousness in a vise-like claw.

"Hey! What—did you—just do?!" Panicking, Luchiriano tried to drag his awareness back to his real body, but for some reason he couldn't break the connection. Luchiriano gurgled out a scream at the unpleasant feeling of pressure, which should've been impossible to feel.

"Can you please answer my question?" the dhampir asked.

Rather than answer, Luchiriano continued to try and resist, but the act of transferring his consciousness to the Living Dead also meant he couldn't use any magic.

"I . . . I'm an adventurer," Luchiriano stuttered. "I used this Living Dead to gather information on these orcs." With no idea what else this new threat could do to him, he decided to simply tell the truth.

". . . Tell me more."

Vandal heard from Luchiriano how the lord of this region, Viscount Valchez, and the Milg Shield Kingdom Marshal Count Palpapekk already knew of the existence of Bugogan's settlement and his ambitions to attack the humans. When the adventurer got into the topic of Count Palpapekk putting together a large force to come and resolve the problem, Vandal's throbbing headache immediately returned.

He had thought that getting rid of the Noble Orc would allow the ghouls to live safely in this demon barren. Once the orcs were taken out, Zadilis and the ghouls would become the top of the food chain. Adventurers would still come, of course, but no more than a handful of parties at once, and not with any frequency. They might lose some individual ghouls, but they would never face a threat big enough to wipe out the entire grotto.

But those assumptions collapsed upon learning that the humans already knew about Bugogan. Not just any humans, but some of the highest-ranking in the nation, who were putting together a plan to send in a large-scale force to wipe the orcs out.

"If the marshal learns the Noble Orcs have been wiped out, will he call off that plan?" Vandal asked.

Luchiriano's Living Dead face tensed for a moment of silence, and then Luchiriano gave up and spoke.

"I'm just an adventurer. I'm not in command, and I don't make the decisions. But I don't think the marshal will cancel the plan," Luchiriano admitted.

Vandal gave a sigh. Just as he expected.

The Noble Orcs, the monsters who posed a direct threat to human society, had met their end today. The other orcs in leadership positions, such as generals and mages, had been wiped out too. Even if some orcs and slave goblins or kobolts had escaped, they wouldn't pose much of a threat.

However, for Marshal Palpapekk and Viscount Valchez, the situation was far more simple. The threat had simply changed from coming from orcs to ghouls.

They would see a ghoul army, led by a Ghoul King, that had just defeated a horde of more than 500 monsters led by multiple rank 6 or higher Noble Orcs. It seemed likely that such a ghoul army would go on to become a terrible threat to human society.

For humans, ghouls and orcs were pretty much the same thing: monsters. Having a horde of hundreds of them in a demon barren just three days from town was a clear threat, nothing less. Not to mention, if they learned that the group also had a dhampir, it was highly likely that the Alda religion would get involved. High Priest Goldan was a clergyman who specialized in killing vampires, after all.

For Vandal, that might create an opportunity to take revenge on the high priest for the murder of his mother. But he still wasn't confident that he had the strength to pull that off.

When he put Dalshia to the stake, Goldan had apparently been the equivalent of a grade B adventurer. If that was true, then Goldan could have fought the rank 7 Bugogan one-on-one with an almost surefire chance to defeat him. He wouldn't have needed to use the kind of tactic Vandal resorted to.

That meant Vandal would have trouble defeating him, unless he got exceptionally lucky. Luck, meanwhile, was the one thing he never seemed to have much of. So he had no hesitation in passing up this chance. In fact, he wanted to bury it in the ground as quickly as possible.

The question is how.

He fixated on Luchiriano's face with his oddly colored eyes. This man was temporarily moving his awareness to this Living Dead familiar and sharing its senses. His body was elsewhere, far away in the town. So Vandal had no way to shut the guy up.

Luchiriano was speaking now, and telling the truth, because of his terror at not being able to escape. But that was all Vandal could do—prevent the man's awareness from leaving the Living Dead. In order to do so, he had to keep his spirit body arm inserted into the Living Dead, meaning he couldn't keep it up forever. There was no question of holding him here, going without rest or sleep, until the man's body died of starvation.

The remaining options were to appeal to his emotions, try to buy him off, or threaten him in order to keep his mouth shut.

The emotional angle wasn't going to work. Vandal didn't know much about the guy, but he did know Luchiriano was here because he'd been paid to be. It didn't matter if he was the greatest philanthropist who ever lived. If he reneged on his contract, keeping quiet about Vandal and the ghouls, and the adventurers' guild found out, he could be punished—or even have a bounty put on his head. He wasn't going to risk that.

Buying him off wouldn't work either. No matter what Vandal promised him, Luchiriano would prefer to receive his above-board payment from the noble offering it to him. There was no reason to risk anything else.

The remaining option was to threaten him, but that was unlikely to be effective. Luchiriano was scared of Vandal in that moment, but once he returned to his body, Vandal wouldn't be able to touch him again. He could try and threaten him verbally, but Vandal was confident that would have the opposite effect.

What adult is going to be scared by a threat from an infant child?

Although in reality, his abnormal appearance and creepy atmosphere were pretty scary.

Realizing that trying to bury this information was impossible, Vandal returned to his first question.

"Now I understand why you are inside this person," Vandal said. "Did you kill this woman?"

The Living Dead looked young and healthy prior to being captured by the orcs. There were no signs of having suffered life-threatening injuries. That meant she had to have been killed on purpose.

Luchiriano realized what he was being asked—whether he killed this woman specifically to turn her into his Living Dead—and shook his head.

"No!" Luchiriano protested. "I don't know why this woman died! I only turned a corpse the lord acquired into this Living Dead!"

"Is that true?" Vandal asked the original owner of the body, but she simply repeated that her body was stolen, and asked for it to be returned.

There was no hope of a reply there. It had been over a month since she died, and she had been forced to watch Bugogan pleasuring himself with her body for most of the time since. It wasn't a surprise that she had lost her mind.

". . . Very well. I will let you go. But if I see you again, you are dead."

Vandal released his hand, and Luchiriano's awareness immediately left the Living Dead.

The scared expression vanished from the face of the Living Dead, and it stopped moving altogether. Vandal thought for a moment it had returned to being a corpse, but it was still breathing, and still had a pulse. It would remain Living Dead even after the one controlling it departed, at least until the remaining MP was consumed.

Thank you. You took back my body, the spirit said.

"No problem. What do you want to do now?" Vandal asked.

What do you mean? I'm already dead. I don't have a future . . .

"And you don't want to be reborn?"

What? What do you mean? Everyone who dies received a new life from god and is reincarnated, the spirit said.

Here on Ramda, people believed in reincarnation. They didn't know the name Rodocolte, but everyone was aware that something allowed dead souls to be reincarnated. She believed that she would now cross to the world of the dead, and eventually come back in a new life. She was therefore unsure why Vandal was asking.

"What I want to ask is, do you want to be reborn right now and have a fresh life?" Vandal asked.

Right now? You can do that?

"Yes. I can't bring you back to life. But it just so happens that there's a new life growing inside you."

Vandal had realized that there was a tiny life, too small to even call a fetus, growing inside the slumped-over Living Dead. So he asked her if she wanted to be reborn as that life.

You want me to become an orc?!

The effects of Death Attribute Allure and the chance to get back her body had kept her friendly, but she was definitely put off by Vandal's suggestion. Being reborn as the child—the orcish child—of the creature that had defiled her, even if after death, was asking a lot. If Vandal had asked her to choose between crossing over or being reborn as an orc, she would have chosen to cross over in an instant.

"Don't worry. I'll remove as much of the orc influence as I can. You won't end up an orc," Vandal assured her.

Can you do that? Any orc blood means the child will always become an orc.

"I can do it. I have some experience with these things." This experience included experiments with enhancing animals, plants, and humans. He knew that death attribute magic could do such things.

On Origin, they had conducted experiments to create mutations by using death attribute magic to kill off certain genetic elements, and those experiments had proven successful. For example, he had erased the mule elements of a donkey and mule crossbreed, ending up with a pure donkey. With seeds, he crossbred one seed resistant to sickness and cold but weak to heat with a different seed resistant to heat but weak to sickness and cold, then shaved off the unnecessary parts to create a type that was resistant to sickness, cold, and heat all at once. The same things could be done with the zygote formed in cattle or humans through the meeting of sperm and egg, and he had achieved successful results in over ninety percent of cases.

These experiments allowed the military nation that owned the lab holding Vandal to expand into the agriculture and livestock industries. It also allowed them to become a center of medicine that eradicated many diseases. *I don't know what happened after I died, of course,* Vandal thought.

He kept that dark history to himself, and continued his explanation in order to put her at ease.

"It would be perfect if applied immediately prior to or after the egg receives the sperm. In this case it has already been implanted in the womb and a little time has passed, so I won't be able to make a perfect human. But I'll make a child so close to a human you won't believe it's actually a Noble Orc."

Like a beastman, she asked.

". . . I've never seen one of those, so I can't say for sure," Vandal replied.

She fell silent for a moment, giving it some serious thought.

Vandal just waited for her to reply. He wasn't doing this simply out of the goodness of his heart. It suited his purposes if she selected to be reborn. Vandal's goals were to get his revenge, to survive his inevitable encounter with the cheaters once they were reincarnated in this world, and to revive his mother Dalshia. As one of the means of achieving that, Vandal was considering a synthetic rebirth, by having Dalshia's spirit possess a highly receptive egg.

Dalshia's body had been reduced to ash, meaning it would be difficult to find a zygote that was receptive to her spirit. It probably wasn't a realistic method, in the end, but there was no harm in keeping as many options on the table as possible.

Of course, things might not work here in Ramda like they did in Origin. Vandal didn't know if the creatures here had genetics or DNA, or if everything functioned the same as it did on Origin. So he wanted to use this woman as an experiment.

That was why Vandal said nothing in reply, and simply waited. If he said anything more, the effects of his Death Attribute Allure skill would ensure that she agreed. But he also didn't want to lie.

Yes, it was hypocritical. He recognized that, which was why he was planning to help her, no matter how things turned out.

Okay then, she eventually said. *I've decided. Please let me be reborn.*

"Very well. I'll do my best," Vandal replied.

He applied the Spirit Bodification to his arms again and sank them into her lower body. Then he passed MP through the small fetus inside the womb of the body, testing the waters to see what kind of condition it was in.

He could feel almost no humanity from the fetus at all. It was essentially a Noble Orc and would completely turn into one if it came to term in this state. As Vandal had already estimated, orc and Noble Orc reproduction was different from other races, with the fetus discarding all non-orc elements from the mother's side.

All he needed to do, then, was swap that relationship around. He applied death attribute MP to the Noble Orc elements to weaken them, while preventing the human elements from becoming weaker in order to bolster them. Then he just needed to prevent the fetus from dying, and the child would be born as something close to a human.

Glad I learned that Magic Control skill, Vandal thought. It was still exceptionally difficult without all the lab equipment. He couldn't just muscle through this procedure with his MP. If he took that approach, he might crush the fragile fetus. He had to carefully, delicately remove each of the unwanted elements.

"All done," he said. "See you again soon."

He placed the spirit of the woman—whose name he didn't even know—inside the fetus. He recalled how on Earth, there had been debate about when the fetus obtained a soul. Was it at the zygote stage, when it became a fetus, or the moment it was born from its mother? The timing of obtaining a soul here, on Ramda, in this specific case, was in this very moment, Vandal meaninglessly pondered.

Then he gave the Living Dead some additional MP. He didn't know how much Luchiriano had already given it, and he didn't want it dying before the baby was born.

Now he just had to decide what to do with the rest of the female adventurers.

"King, why you so popular?" a ghoul asked him.

"Probably thanks to my skills," Vandal replied. The female adventurers had been gathering around him since before he even started questioning Luchiriano.

"Ugh . . ."

"Please . . . please . . ."

He was surrounded by semi-naked women, so ghouls passing by considered it popularity, but the truth was different. These women were little more than living corpses now, minds reduced to shells of their former selves, and wishing only for death. The death attribute magic that swirled around Vandal therefore looked to them like nothing but death himself, come to save them from this hell.

The Death Attribute Allure skill shouldn't have had any effect on living people, but it seemed to work on anyone alive who was earnestly wishing for death.

The women waited for Vandal to kill them, but it was chipping away at Vandal's own mental state to be surrounded by people desperate for him to take their lives. When talking to the spirit and performing the resulting operation, his desire to avoid looking at the women around him had actually helped him focus.

That said, not looking at them wasn't going to make them go away. The ghouls were waiting for their king to make a decision.

"First off, I'm not going to kill them." For Vandal, these Milg Shield Kingdom adventurers were his enemies, but he wasn't going to kill them when they were in such a state as this. "Releasing them close to a town—"

"No!" one of them screamed.

"Don't do it! Kill me, kill me!" cried another.

"—wouldn't work," Vandal concluded. He didn't have an understanding of the state of the world like Luchiriano, but he was well aware that releasing them in this state would mark their ends. He figured they might have family, loved ones, and others waiting for them to come back, but they weren't acting like they did. Maybe they had no one, maybe they didn't get along with their family, and maybe their fellow adventurers had already gotten killed by the orcs.

That said, keeping them in the grotto was out of the question. They were under Vandal's thrall at the moment, but that might not last once they recovered the will to live. Rather, his skill losing all effect was highly likely. When they returned to sanity, they might also return to being adventurers. To being his enemies.

He felt bad for the female adventurers, but for Vandal, the ghouls had to come first.

"In that case . . . do you want to become ghouls?"

That seemed like the next natural thing to ask. Zadilis had told him about a ritual that could be used to turn human women into ghouls. Talea was one example of that in action.

"Become ghouls?"

"Yes. To become my brethren—"

Before Vandal had even finished speaking, light glittered again in the dead eyes of one of the female adventurers.

"I'll do it. I'll become a ghoul."

Her eyes sparkled like those of a carnivore faced with fresh prey. She was smiling, but rather than smiling at the hope of being saved, it was more like she was so broken that she had been cut free from her former self altogether.

"Me too. Make me a ghoul . . ."

"I'll do it. I'll be your brethren . . ."

All the female adventurers desired to become ghouls, so Vandal acquired thirteen new brethren.

"The boy did well, getting those adventurers to agree to become ghouls," Zadilis said. "If they could return to human society, that would be one thing, but without that possibility . . . welcoming them into our race is all we can do."

"True. He was talking to one of them for quite a while. It looked like he used some magic on them too."

Zadilis and Basdia had been watching Vandal from a short distance away, waiting for the right moment to let the female adventurers know that becoming ghouls was an option.

"I noticed that," Zadilis said. "Since they finished talking, that same woman hasn't moved at all. It's like she's dead. Once things calm down, I'll ask him about it."

The women looked like ghosts, reaching toward Vandal as though he were a single shaft of light piercing down for them from the heavens. Zadilis decided to give them a little longer to recover.

On a refreshing morning in February, the chill morning breeze was mixed with the smell of blood.

Then a loud, wild shout rang out. The ghouls, busy removing the internal organs from some orc, goblin, and kobolt bodies for breakfast, turned to look at the source of the scream and saw Vigaro looking up at the morning sun.

"Hey, did Vigaro get bigger?!" one of them asked.

"Has he ranked up?!"

Vigaro used to be over six feet tall, but now he looked bigger than that. His lion head looked fiercer, his fangs thicker, his body stronger, his limbs bunched with more muscle while retaining their flexibility. He looked like something that was considered little more than a myth among the ghouls, and that hadn't been seen here in these demon barrens for hundreds of years.

"A berserker! He's a Ghoul Berserker!"

Vigaro had been a veteran Ghoul Barbarian. During the intense fighting the previous night, he had killed multiple Orc Generals around the same level of basic strength as him, and a Noble Orc, which was a whole rank higher. All that experience, combined with increasing his skill levels, meant he met the conditions for ranking up.

While he still hadn't reached the truly legendary rank of Ghoul Tyrant, the ghouls were happy to chant Vigaro's name, witnessing the birth of a Ghoul Berserker capable of defeating one hundred human soldiers alone.

Five minutes later, Vandal was receiving an early morning lecture from three beautiful women. Some might have been jealous of the attention, but from his point of view, this was far from a reward.

"Listen, boy," said Zadilis. "You are our leader, but that doesn't mean you need to fight the enemy leader in mortal combat."

"We might have only got in the way when fighting the Noble Orc—maybe—but there was no reason for you to suddenly fly off alone," Basdia chimed in. "If you had taken some reinforcements with you, and had backup from the start, you wouldn't have needed to rely on such a dangerous strategy!"

They are right! When Sam told me what happened, I thought I might pass out! Vandal, you are still a baby! You aren't even three years old. That was far too reckless of you!

Dalshia was laying into him the hardest, but he was the only one who could see her and hear her voice, so from Zadilis and Basdia's perspective, it was a two-woman berating.

"Yes, I'm sorry."

Vandal didn't make excuses. He just apologized. When he thought back over it now, charging in to fight Bugogan alone had been reckless. Surely there had been a better way. He had to accept the worry he had caused Zadilis and Basdia, and especially his mother.

As Basdia had suggested, they should probably have all attacked Bugogan together. Vandal could have focused on holding him in place while the ghouls used bows, missile weapons, and magic to whittle him down. It might have taken a while, but they likely could have neutralized him. Prior to starting the attack, he simply had to apply some Virulent Poison to the ghouls' arrows and missiles. It would have been hard to ensure zero deaths, but in terms of overall difficulty, it would have been around the same level as letting himself almost lose a lung. After a night to cool down and think things over, he saw these potential strategies. The reason he hadn't seen them at the time was because, although he hadn't been aware of this, he had been in something of a panic.

It had been a while since he had been in a real battle, and never one on that scale, so it was probably inevitable. He simply steeled himself to face the rest of this lecture.

It just shows how much you care for the ghouls, of course, so that's enough. This time. Just don't do it again! Dalshia finally seemed to be wrapping up.

"It's also true that we weren't strong enough for you to fall back on us, Van," Basdia admitted. "I fired my own bow at that Noble Orc, but his magic sword chopped all of my arrows down. We couldn't back you up. We couldn't even make an opening! Sorry, Van. We basically forced you to do something reckless."

"That's true," Zadilis agreed. "Thanks to you, boy, not a single ghoul died. All because you shared your magic items, enhanced us with your skills, shared your MP, and took care of the enemy magicians. From that point of view, we've been asking too much of you from the beginning. My apologies, boy."

". . . Huh?" Vandal had been expecting the chewing-out to continue, but Dalshia forgave him almost at once, and Basdia and Zadilis then started to actually apologize to him.

Surprised, he waited for the other shoe to drop, but no "gotcha!" moment was forthcoming. They seemed to mean it.

"Is that it?" Vandal couldn't help but ask for confirmation. Dalshia and the others blinked.

"I think so. You don't want us to berate you, do you?" Zadilis asked, puzzled at Vandal's question.

The baby proceeded to answer without thinking. "No, of course not, but when I've been chewed out like this in the past, it lasted for a lot longer." In his previous lives on Earth and Origin, Vandal had not been blessed with the adults he had to deal with.

When the uncle who raised him on Earth had scolded him, it had comprised a menu of violence and shouting. He was a man concerned about appearances, and so rather than scold Vandal on the spot, he had always waited until they got home. He never listened to Vandal's side of things, never considered why things might have happened like they did, offered no advice other than "don't ever do that again," and never considered what he might do to prevent a relapse once the scolding was finished. These scoldings came from a place of anger at having to deal with Vandal's perceived slights when, from his uncle's perspective, he was just trying to raise the poor orphan in a semblance of luxury. But all Vandal took away from these scoldings were anger and fear.

When his aunt scolded him, it lasted forever. Vandal had no idea what it was she really wanted to say as she droned on in a dismal tone. She continued until she was sated, or something else to do came up. At its worst, she continued for hours, and then further berated him for wasting her time.

His schoolteachers had always blamed Vandal first whenever there was trouble. Rather than consider who had caused it, or what the reasons were, it was easiest for them to just make the weird kid with the tatty old uniform the bad guy. That actually worked at elementary school, keeping the class in check, so Vandal thought such treatment was normal at school.

He had put those lessons into practice at junior and high school, seeking to become little more than thin air, blending in completely and spending his time peacefully as a result.

On Origin, getting "scolded" meant being punished. There, Vandal was a human lab rat. The researchers who raised him hadn't seen him as something to educate, but something to train. Fists turned into electric shocks, the lectures so pointed that they practically eviscerated him. Of course, his captors had no reason to listen to him, and everything was conducted to put their needs first.

In the most extreme cases, they left him convulsing on the floor with electric shocks even after he did everything they told him to, as part of an experiment to see if unexpected, illogical pain changed the nature of his magical power. All of these experiences—indeed, all of this trauma—had left Vandal terribly afraid of making anyone angry. If it was someone he could kill without consequence or someone he wanted to kill, it didn't bother him. He wasn't scared of killing or having to fight to the death. But he didn't want anyone else to scold him or get mad at him.

Of course, he didn't think Dalshia, Zadilis, or Basdia were going to start acting like his aunt, uncle, or those researchers. But he tried to avoid upsetting them regardless.

Vandal, I'm sorry. I'm so sorry if I scared you, Dalshia said. She knew most of Vandal's past and could probably guess most of the rest, and she gave him a hug with her spirit body arms. They couldn't physically touch him, but he felt a slight chill.

No need for you to apologize, mom, Vandal said. This was trauma from a previous life, so it was unfair for his mom to take it into consideration. She was the first mother in this world to even raise a child with memories of a former life, so there wasn't really anything to take notes from.

But the other two didn't know anything about his memories of a previous life, so they could only come to false conclusions.

"Boy, I've never asked much about your mother . . ." Zadilis started.

"What was she like?" Basdia asked. "What was she like normally . . . and what was she like when she got angry?"

Vandal saw sympathy in their eyes, and noticed an awkward tone to their voices. After a moment, he realized they thought his mother had abused him.

"No, no, this isn't about my mother. This seems like a good chance to explain things. Can you ask Vigaro to join us?"

Vandal, you don't need to worry about me, Dalshia said. *They can't even see me.*

I do worry about you, Vandal replied. *It makes me sad that they've got the wrong idea about you.*

He didn't want the ghouls to think badly of Dalshia, and he had been wanting to explain everything to them anyway. This seemed like a good opportunity to explain everything.

"I see. Very interesting."

Vandal explained that he had lived previous lives, that he

had his memories from them, and that he had lived them on different worlds. He explained that one hundred people with superpowers that Vandal himself had not been given were going to be reborn in this world.

His ghoulish audience was surprised, but also quickly accepting. That was better than them not believing him at all, but they had believed him so easily that it threw Vandal off a little.

Then they explained the reasons why.

"You are a small child with over one hundred million MP that can use never-before-seen attribute magic," Zadilis said. "Even taking into account the fact you are a dhampir, having such a history is actually the least crazy explanation."

"Not to mention, you know far too much for being not even three years old. Sam and his daughters couldn't have taught you all that. If that was knowledge from a previous life, that makes more sense," Basdia agreed.

"As they say," Vigaro said. "I have nothing to add."

". . . I figured you wouldn't."

"It's a surprise that there will be one hundred more of you coming, boy."

"One hundred more people with one hundred million MP," Basdia pondered. The ghouls looked worried about a bunch of boys and girls with so much MP showing up, becoming adventurers or state-employed knights and magicians and then coming to the demon barrens on a hunting trip.

Vandal shook his head. "No, I think they'll have a lot less MP than me."

"What? Are you sure?" Basdia asked.

"Yes. The reason I have so much MP is because I didn't get anything else."

Everyone other than Vandal had received cheat abilities and attribute magic aptitude from Rodocolte. The reason Vandal had massive MP was because he didn't have anything else. Rodocolte had said this "empty space" would fill up with MP. To borrow that terminology, the other one hundred wouldn't have that same "empty space." That would be filled with the goodies that Vandal hadn't received.

Most of them would likely have around 10,000 MP, which was the average for the best magicians in Ramda. Vandal shared that observation with the ghouls, and they breathed audible sighs.

"Okay. That's a relief," Zadilis said.

"They still have cheat abilities, you know!" Vandal protested.

"I don't know what you classify as a 'cheat,' boy, but you are pretty out of the ordinary with one hundred million MP," Zadilis replied.

She made a good point. The greatest magicians in Ramda might be lucky to exceed 10,000 MP. Grade A or S adventurers, who were considered beyond human, and powerful monsters that even they might not be able to defeat could reach 100,000 MP. More than one hundred million was a volume alongside the gods or demon king of myth.

"You think so? I mean, if I could use normal attribute magic, maybe."

The actual holder of all that power still wasn't feeling it. He couldn't use fire or earth attribute magic, the stuff that was useful in battle, and his magic control was still so poor he had to drop a couple thousand MP to use a single spell. He didn't consider his own strength to be a cheat whatsoever.

I think you should have a little more self-confidence, Dalshia offered.

"Hmmm. I'll do my best," Vandal replied. "In any case, I'm not sure I should remain Ghoul King. Those being reborn here are coming from worlds that only have humans, so we can't be sure how they'll react."

This world had systems like status and skills that were akin to video games on Earth and Origin. If they saw monsters, they might just start killing them.

Still, wiping out monsters wouldn't be such a problem. The problem would be their treatment of Vida's new races, which were treated as monsters by the Amidd Empire. That went double for the ghouls, of course, who weren't even treated as one of Vida's races. If Vandal's classmates found out the ghouls were Vandal's allies, they might just go to town on all of them, including the women and children.

Vandal and the other one hundred were not, when considered rationally, on opposite sides. They weren't enemies. Rodocolte's original mistake and some subsequent bad luck meant they didn't realize Vandal was also on Origin, and that they had ended up finishing off his undead existence.

That said, after they killed him on Origin, he had said some pretty inflammatory stuff to Rodocolte, including that he would kill them all. He couldn't be sure how they would react to that. They might be connected because they were all reincarnated, but Vandal wouldn't jump at the chance of becoming friends with someone who had sworn to kill him. Vandal could hope that Rodocolte was still watching him and realized that he no longer felt so intent on his vengeance . . . but the chances of that seemed slim.

He certainly didn't watch over us much when we were on Origin, Vandal thought. Had he been watching, he might have slipped Hiroto Amemiya and the others a little divine intervention to save Vandal. That had never happened, and so Vandal held little hope for aid from Rodocolte.

Now that the Noble Orcs had been wiped out, Vandal therefore thought it best to return the title they had given him, but the ghouls had a different outlook.

"Hmm," Zadilis said. "You might be right, but those one hundred won't be coming all at once, will they? They'll arrive in the order they die in that other world, Origin, correct? This is all still some point in the future. Even if they do appear together, it should only be a few at a time."

When they had killed Vandal on Origin, they looked to be around their early twenties. But they also had dangerous jobs, such as dealing with an undead outbreak from a secret military facility. If they fumbled a job like that, one of them might die— six months later, or a year, perhaps.

They not only had the cheat abilities that Vandal hadn't received, but they also had aptitude for magic and the protection of luck and fate. They weren't going to die easily. The science on Origin was also somewhat more advanced than on Earth, due to the extra element of magic. So long as they weren't murdered or fell prey to serious illnesses like cancer, they might live for eighty or even one hundred years on Origin.

That was "some point" in the future, for sure. Vandal also agreed no more than a few of them—at most—were going to die at the same time.

"We also don't know all one hundred of them will be born in the Amidd Empire or its nations. They might arrive in the nations you are heading to, beyond the mountains, or on different continents. They might not be born to human parents. They could be ghouls or other Vida races," Zadilis said.

"Sure, that's all possible . . ." Vandal admitted.

Zadilis was making sense, but Vandal couldn't finish his thought. Then Basdia stepped in.

"We also face threats other than just those one hundred. If the humans send grade B or A adventurers to this demon barren, that alone could wipe us out. Or high-ranking monsters from other demon barrens may come here and build their strength again, like the Noble Orc. Just those one hundred turning up isn't reason enough for you to leave us, Vandal."

As Basdia pointed out, the ghouls had become the most powerful force in this demon barren. But if the Milg Shield Kingdom started to send in high-grade adventurers, they wouldn't last long.

"We wouldn't have won this battle without you, Vandal," Basdia said. "Even if we could've, we wouldn't have been able to have the kids to replace our losses. We can't worry about something decades in the future."

"Yes, I can see . . . where you are coming from," Vandal admitted. He didn't really have an argument against any of that. Basdia and the ghouls faced threats every day, and for them, it was normal to fight rather than run to survive, prepare rather than cower in fear.

"If those one hundred start hunting monsters, it will be worse for us if you leave, Van. We would be better off with you here."

"Ah! I didn't even think of that!" Vandal admitted, a little surprised. It was highly likely the one hundred would begin hunting monsters even if Vandal wasn't involved with them. After all, they would have the strength, and in Ramda, monsters were evil. Hunting them would fulfill his classmates' sense of justice and fast-track them to money and fame.

The final opinion—and the one that knocked Vandal out for the count—came from, unexpectedly, Vigaro.

"Anyway. They can't be strong as you, Vandal."

This comment made Vandal's mouth drop open. Of course they were stronger. They would have strength beyond common sense, powerful enough that they were basically cheating. It was silly to suggest they weren't as strong as him.

"Th-they are stronger," Vandal replied. "They have to be. I'm sure of it."

"But they die. They can die. So you can kill," Vigaro said.

He made it sound so obvious that Vandal reflexively tried to respond. "That makes no—oh!"

But then Vandal realized something. Vigaro was right—they could die.

Rodocolte had given the one hundred cheat-level abilities. They were protected by fortune and guided by fate, yes.

But Rodocolte's ultimate aim, after their deaths on Earth, was to use them to develop Ramda. He had sent them to Origin first simply to gain some experience. That was why they would be reincarnated in Ramda in the order that they died.

Which meant they had to be able to die. If they couldn't die in Origin, then they would never arrive in Ramda. That meant Rodocolte wouldn't have given them cheat powers such as being unable to die or be killed. They might have cheat abilities that gave them incredible attack strength, but so long as they had standard defenses, then he could kill them.

Maybe they could move at incredible speeds, but he could make them sick with Generate Sickness. Maybe they could regenerate severed limbs instantaneously, but taking out the brain or heart in a single blow would surely still kill them. They might have impenetrable defenses, but he could use Old Age to age them out of the game.

None of these things were easy to do. He would have to risk his life to win.

But Vandal, he had death attribute magic. Magic that allowed him to control death when mastered, bringing it closer or pushing it further away. If his opponents would eventually die, that meant there was a means to kill them, and that Vandal could find a way to trigger it.

"I wonder why I never realized such a fundamental truth before."

"Only natural to fear thing you don't have," Vigaro said.

"Not to mention, they killed you once already. Fair for you to believe you can't defeat them," Zadilis added.

Vandal dropped to his knees. The two of them had hit the jackpot in terms of why he was scared of the one hundred.

"I've been thinking about this for three years, ever since I was born, and I never saw it like this," Vandal said. "Thank you for pointing all of this out. You have given me new hope."

"You and minions help us. No trouble," Vigaro said, with a satisfied smile through fangs that were considerably bigger than yesterday's.

It was clear Vandal wasn't going to be allowed to give back his crown.

"But we might get in your way if you really want to become an adventurer or noble," Zadilis said.

"I'll convince people I tamed you. If that doesn't work, I'll just accrue enough power so that they can't ignore me," Vandal reasoned.

"You've made progress today, Van," Basdia said.

He had his own cheat abilities and could kill using them. That reduced half the issues Vandal felt he was facing in his life. His head felt much clearer.

He still had his goal of getting revenge on High Priest Goldan and Heinz, but he was sure he could do that once he became stronger. Earth and Origin were one thing. Here, he could actually see his own skills, and he had more than one hundred million MP to use them. If he could master that power, he could surely get his revenge and kill the cheaters.

It felt as if the rugged mountains and valleys that lay ahead in his life had suddenly fallen flat.

Feeling much better, Vandal remembered something he had been planning to say that morning.

"Oh, by the way. The humans were also preparing to wipe out the orc settlement, and they now know we beat them to it. Should we do something about it?"

"Boy," sighed Zadilis. "You really buried the far more pressing concern."

So the meeting of the minds had to go on.

Name: Vigaro
Rank: 6
Race: Ghoul Berserker
Level: 5
Job: None
Job Level: 100

Job History: None

Age: 168

——Passive Skills

[Night Vision] [Brute Strength: Level 4] [Resist Pain: Level 4] [Paralytic Venom (Claws): Level 1]

——Active Skills

[Axe Proficiency: Level 5 (UP!)] [Brawling Proficiency: Level 2] [Command: Level 3] [Cooperation: Level 2]

Name: Basdia

Rank: 4

Race: Ghoul Warrior

Level: 63

Job: None

Job Level: 100

Job History: None

Age: 26

——Passive Skills

[Night Vision] [Brute Strength: Level 3] [Resist Pain: Level 2] [Paralytic Venom (Claws): Level 3]

——Active Skills

[Axe Proficiency: Level 3] [Shield Proficiency: Level 2] [Bow Proficiency: Level 2]

[Thrown Projectile Proficiency: Level 1] [Sneaking Steps: Level 1] [Cooperation: Level 2]

——Maladies

[Infertile]

Luchiriano, looking pale and sickly, was having a tense morning.

"That concludes my report," he said. Kneeling before his master, the mustached Viscount Velnoh Valchez, and a whole bunch of knights, Luchiriano had delivered his report.

On the throne sat a man who was well into his middle age. He was plump, moderately sized, and not normally the kind of person Luchiriano would have been nervous around. Luchiriano might not specialize in combat, but he had gone before nobles to receive jobs from them many times. But every time Luchiriano stood before this man, he felt a spine-chilling, distasteful tension.

"Is that report to be believed?" the man asked.

"Yes, Marshal Palpapekk," Valchez said.

The man's name was Marshal Thomas Palpapekk. He held the rank of count because the Milg Shield Kingdom belonged to the Amidd Empire, where the emperor bestowed ranks upon all nobles. If the Milg Shield Kingdom had been its own isolated kingdom, he had proven himself capable enough to at least hold the position of duke. He was a marshal who knew how to do his job.

Since Palpapekk assumed his position, the Milg Shield Kingdom had repelled the attacks of the Olbaum Electorate Kingdom, enhanced its internal stability, and cooperated with adventurers to wipe out monsters from the demon barrens, preventing all sorts of disasters before they even had a chance to occur.

"I see. The Noble Orcs have been wiped out, and their minions scattered," the marshal said.

"This is extremely good news, isn't it, Lord Marshal?" Viscount Valchez offered. He did look very happy, offering a smile to Marshal Palpapekk. His bristling mustache almost seemed to glow. He was clearly relieved that he wasn't going to have to spend all those taxes on hiring a bunch of adventurers, and also send in soldiers and knights, likely for many of them to die. Nobles had a reputation of callously using up those beneath them, but it was only the really twisted—or stupid—ones who did that. Once nobles reached a certain level of capability, they did their best to avoid casualties rather than create them.

Soldiers were required to keep the peace, and if they died, replacements weren't exactly available on the spot. They weren't security guards, who could be paid and used as required. Permanent soldiers needed to be trained and kept loyal.

That went double for those knights who had served nobles for many years. If they were callously whittled away, they would quickly lose faith in their noble masters and might even go looking for a better lord to serve.

Preventing deaths among soldiers conscripted from among the peasants was just as important. Losing too many of their young, robust workforce would reduce the productivity of the region, potentially causing economic issues. A dissatisfied populace was never a good thing.

The case was slightly different for adventurers. They were generally responsible for all of their own work, so losing ten or even twenty of them had little negative effects in a city as large as one overseen by Viscount Valchez. Hundreds of adventurers died annually in the Milg Shield Kingdom, but no one said that was the responsibility of the rulers.

But when considered nationally, suddenly losing a large number of adventurers in a single region would affect the handling of monsters in the demon barrens, preventing the circulation of materials obtained by adventurers, and negatively influencing monster policy and the economy.

Furthermore, adventurers rarely put down roots. If rumors started up about a lord forcing reckless quests on adventurers, they might simply stop working for that lord. That would have a long-term negative effect on regional management.

Therefore, it was better to have no sacrifices, or as few as possible. Of course, in some cases risks had to be taken—such as when facing down 500 monsters led by a Noble Orc with designs to conquer human cities. The removal of that threat, with no need to put together a force to fight them, was great news for Viscount Valchez. Defeating a powerful monster would have offered glory, but he wasn't interested.

Marshal Palpapekk, however, had a different take on the situation.

"You are being shortsighted, Viscount Valchez," the marshal said. "Indeed, we should probably increase the size of the planned party . . . and even ask for aid from High Priest Goldan, with his extensive knowledge of hunting vampires."

"What?! Why do you think such a thing, Lord Marshal? The Noble Orcs are gone! The threat has been eradicated!" Valchez exclaimed.

"Eradicated? Nothing of the sort. The threat has just shifted—from orcs to ghouls. A group of ghouls capable of victory against a horde of 500 monsters, led by Noble Orcs. Luchiriano couldn't confirm, but they likely have a Ghoul Mage . . . and maybe even higher-ranked monsters, such as a High Mage or Berserker. You think such a group won't be a threat to us?"

For humans, ghouls were like orcs—just another monster. The only real differences were that they had females, so they didn't need to take human women in order to procreate, and they rarely left the demon barrens. One of Viscount Valchez's knights proceeded to speak up along these lines.

"Respectfully, Lord Marshal, there has never been a confirmed group of ghouls active outside a demon barren. Doesn't that suggest that this group will at least never come out to trouble us?" the knight asked. "The ghouls from the demon barren in question are particularly reserved. They rarely even fight adventurers. As this adventurer reported to us, the Noble Orcs were also using ghoul women for breeding. Surely this incident is purely the ghouls' revenge on the orcs?"

A bunch of ghouls with the strength to defeat Noble Orcs and their horde was a threat, that was true. But if the fighting was simply for survival inside the demon barren, it was unlikely to spread outside. No need for the humans to get involved in conflicts that they couldn't even see.

Marshal Palpapekk gave a nod, at least acknowledging that opinion. But then he continued, "True, but that's only as we have known ghouls until now. Has there ever been a pack of ghouls led by a dhampir child before?"

"No," Viscount Valchez's knight was forced to admit. "I've never heard of such a thing."

"Not to mention, it is highly likely that this dhampir is a Ghoul King. Correct?" Marshal Palpapekk asked Luchiriano.

"Yes. Considering the circumstances, it seems likely that this dhampir is both the Ghoul King and named Vandal," Luchiriano replied. "Although I cannot be held responsible if the truth somewhat differs."

One of the ghouls had said something about "Vandal" coming, and then the dhampir child appeared. That suggested his name was Vandal. One of the other ghouls said that the king was called "Vandal." The pieces were there, but that wasn't absolute proof that they fit together. While it was hard to believe that a young dhampir—not even a child, but a toddler—led a large group of ghouls as their king, no one spoke up to the contrary of the suggestion. They had nothing that proved otherwise.

Then Marshal Palpapekk made a further, shocking revelation.

"I actually have some idea who this Vandal, this child dhampir, might be."

"You do, my Lord?"

"Is this true, Lord Marshal?!"

It sounded like Marshal Palpapekk's knights hadn't heard this yet either, because they joined Viscount Valchez and his men in exclamations of surprise. Even Luchiriano couldn't help but look up in shock.

"It was about three years ago," the marshal said. "Surely you recall, Viscount Valchez, that dark elf who was wanted across our nation for succumbing to the sinister charms of a vampire. Her name was Dalshia. I had my men look into the situation, and we determined that the name of the vampire involved was Varen. It is hardly rare for parents to combine their own names when naming their child."

The child of Varen and Dalshia, and so "Vandal." A common method among peasants.

"I thought that dhampir was killed!" Viscount Valchez said.

"No. Only his mother, the dark elf, was executed. The dhampir would have only just been born at the time, but its body was never found."

"I can't believe it! The clergy demand such a high price, yet these are the kinds of services they render?"

"Still, half-vampire or not, a newborn infant surely couldn't have survived without its mother. This has to be a coincidence."

"But the ages match up. It is dangerous to write this off so quickly."

Marshal Palpapekk stepped in, his powerful voice cutting off the knights squabbling over their theories.

"We need to beware of the possibility that this Ghoul King Vandal isn't satisfied with simply having survived. If he also seeks revenge."

The knights fell silent, their faces tense.

"I'm sure I don't have to tell you gentlemen what will happen then."

Viscount Valchez looked particularly pale. A group of powerful ghouls, led by a dhampir with an axe to grind. That was clearly a bigger threat than even the Noble Orcs had been.

Orcs were stupid, and even when led by a promoted species, they lacked cooperation, offering plenty of openings to exploit. Ghouls, on the other hand, were much smarter than orcs, and could cooperate better than kobolts. While only mages or higher types of orcs could use magic, almost all female ghouls could use it. They couldn't reproduce as quickly as orcs, but that information was meaningless to the nobles and knights gathered here.

These ghouls had defeated more than 500 orcs. There had to be at least 400 of them. If a group of that size was going to attack, the first target would be Viscount Valchez's domain, which was why his mustache was almost drooping to the ground.

"Please, Lord Marshal! Lend us your strength!" the Viscount exclaimed.

"Of course I will, Viscount Valchez," the marshal said. "We will put together an even larger force at once, and wipe out the ghouls and their dhampir from this demon barren completely."

This decision allowed Marshal Palpapekk to create an even larger eradication party, still under the auspices of a request from the local lord. If this operation was a success, and the marshal could take down a dhampir that even the famous vampire-hunting High Priest Goldan had failed to kill, it would increase his standing even further.

These political machinations mean nothing to me! I just need to get out of here! Luchiriano didn't want to see the face of that dhampir ever again. He hung on desperately until his lord finally dismissed him.

Later the same day, the marshal was situated in his office in the manor where he was staying, fighting a mountain of paperwork.

Normally, the work of putting together a party to hunt some monsters would fall to the lord of the domain in question and the adventurers' guild. However, this was going to be a very large group, including not only adventurers but also soldiers and knights from the national army. The lord of the domain, Viscount Velnoh Valchez, had given Marshal Palpapekk all the authority he needed, and begged for his help.

Of course, Viscount Valchez was pulling his weight too, but Marshal Palpapekk was the one who held the final authority to sign off on all of the documents, and if any mistakes were made, he was the one who would be held responsible. Now they had to deal with the repercussions of the decision made that morning.

Orders to increase the number of army soldiers and knights. Budgeting for the additional equipment those reinforcements would require. Extra rations. Further reconnaissance to send out to watch the demon barrens.

Issues with the adventurers' guild fell under the authority of the commerce minister, not the marshal himself, and so he had to pass everything through his noble minions, adding another peak to the mountain range of papers.

The only saving grace in the situation was that the recent conflict with the Olbaum Electorate Kingdom had concluded in the Amidd Empire's favor, with few casualties, and so they had some room in the budget. Of course, requesting that money meant more documents to read and sign.

"This looks like hard work. I sympathize, Thomas, having to spend your already short life on such pointless pushing of paper."

The voice entered the room, along with cold night air from a window that Palpapekk didn't remember opening. He finished signing the current document and put down his pen.

The marshal looked up to see a single bat.

"If you feel that way, why don't you help me out? If I recall correctly, my friend, you have, what, eternal life?"

"I think I have already helped you plenty. Or have you finally grown disillusioned with the transient glory of human society, and now you want to obtain eternity for yourself?" The bat spoke in a cool and collected tone. Anyone else would probably be surprised by all this—the bat was even using his first name—but the marshal hardly reacted at all.

"No, thank you," the marshal replied. "I've no plans to join your kind, and you surely don't wish for that either. No need to blow smoke, vampire."

The bat was a familiar, sent by a vampire.

Marshal Thomas Palpapekk had been born the second son of Count Palpapekk. They were a military family, long entrusted with powerful forces that protected the religious nation from the Olbaum Electorate Kingdom. Even considering that long and illustrious history, Thomas was an exceptional child.

But exceptional didn't matter as much when he was also the second child. Unless the first child was a complete mess, the second child wasn't going to inherit anything. His older brother wasn't quite in the same league as Thomas, but he was still a capable man. In both letters and in fighting, Thomas had been clearly superior—and both Thomas and his brother had been aware of it. But the difference was also small enough that it wasn't worth breaking the entire system to make Thomas the count.

Whichever brother took the rank of marshal wouldn't change their defenses, or soldiers, or knights. It wouldn't change the ministers who had long served the Count Palpapekk house. Minor skirmishes with the Olbaum Electorate Kingdom had continued, maybe once every few years, but the Milg Shield Kingdom had "shield" in the name for a reason. What the one appointed to marshal had to do was defend, and defend alone. The command of invasions—and the resulting glory—went to the marshal of the Amidd Empire and his generals.

That meant, no matter how superior Thomas proved himself to be, he would never have become count. The only options left for Thomas were marriage into a noble family, a baron or some other noble who had only had daughters, or to become a minister for his brother's household.

That was when the vampire had appeared in front of him.

"Don't you want to be count?" the vampire had asked. "Can you accept that your brother stands over you simply because he was born first?"

They were good points. Soon after the two of them joined forces, the marshal's older brother was killed in an unfortunate—and unavoidable—accident. That was how Thomas became marshal and became the successor of the Palpapekk house.

"Indeed. You see right through me. A human collaborator of your rank is a rare and precious thing," the bat admitted, making it plain that without his title as marshal, the vampire would have no use for Thomas.

The marshal decided to end the small talk there and got down to business.

"You know why I've called you," he said.

"Of course. This dhampir, born to the traitor Varen and the dark elf woman. I graciously shared that information with you, and you still let them get away," the vampire said softly.

Thomas didn't completely understand the vampire factions, but he knew that they were broadly divided into those that followed the evil gods and those that followed the Goddess Vida. This vampire was one that followed the evil gods, but that didn't mean he was planning anything as bold as wiping out humanity.

After the Demon King Gudranis was killed, the remaining evil gods fractured without their leader, and started to act purely in their own interests. Some searched for the sealed flesh of the demon king in order to revive him. Some plotted their revenge on the gods and humans who caused their downfall. Some simply lost themselves in sloth and gluttony. Some departed for other worlds, seeing no hope of conquering this one. There were even those who started to fight the other evil gods for domination and power.

Then there were those who cast aside their original purpose, and simply sought to fulfill their own selfish desires. The vampire Thomas was conversing with now belonged to a group led by just such an evil god. But this particular evil god—and the vampires who followed him—had a variety of reasons to want to hunt down and kill the half-vampire dhampirs.

It wasn't because they considered them evil, exactly. They had more petty reasons. They didn't want dhampirs siding with humans and starting to hunt other vampires; they wanted to maintain the pure and noble vampire race; they wanted to set an example for the other factions. And they enjoyed killing the dhampirs in front of their brethren who had foolishly succumbed to the appeal of love.

In this case, that was the reason.

The master of the bat Thomas was currently conversing with, a vampire whose name and face he didn't know, had been ordered by another vampire higher in the pecking order to kill the dhampir born to the subordinate species Varen and the dark elf. The vampire had managed to kill Varen, but then he had let the pregnant dark elf get away—and not out of mercy.

The vampire wanted to see the dark elf and dhampir baby brutally killed by the humans. That was the kind of display the evil god they worshipped simply adored. He gave Thomas the information on the dhampir to instigate this outcome. But in the end, only the mother—the dark elf—died, and the dhampir remained missing. As it had still been a breastfeeding baby, it had been presumed to have starved to death after the loss of its mother.

But no. It was alive and playing at Ghoul King in a demon barren far from Evbejia. When the vampire had received this information from Thomas, he had experienced a sensation he had practically forgotten—surprise. Then it sent out this bat familiar.

". . . There were a number of unexpected elements," Thomas said, with a pained look on his face as he recalled the events from when they attempted to eliminate the dark elf and its baby.

When Thomas first heard about the dhampir, he passed the information to an up-and-coming adventurer party called Five Hue Blades, planning to give them the glory for the kill. His idea was to form a strong connection with them, give them further quests in the future, and create an image of the Five Hue Blades as the marshal's own exclusive adventurers—with them potentially becoming his own underlings in the future.

However, High Priest Goldan of the Amidd Empire's Divine Alda religion happened to be staying in a village close to Evbejia, a coincidence that invited his interference. The dark elf had also resisted to the last, revealing nothing about the location of the dhampir. This pushed High Priest Goldan to a fever pitch, and ignoring the pleas of Thomas's own minions, the clergyman executed the elf. To make matters worse, once the dark elf was dead, the Five Hue Blades left Evbejia without searching for the dhampir.

That meant Thomas had been forced to leave the search for the dhampir baby in the hands of High Priest Goldan and his minions, over whom the marshal could exert exactly zero control. As a result, the dhampir survived and escaped.

"The most unexpected bit," the vampire said, "is that a breastfeeding baby could avoid the search of the high priest and survive until today."

"Indeed," Thomas said. "On top of that, he is leading some ghouls, and appears to have somehow changed jobs, as he has Medium abilities."

"A Medium? We are talking about a child barely three years old?"

"It's true. An adventurer we hired was using a Living Dead familiar, and the dhampir saw through the technique almost at once."

The marshal, Viscount Valchez, and the other knights all believed that Vandal had seen through the Living Dead because he had a Medium job. They never would have dreamed that Vandal possessed death attribute magic, something that didn't even exist in this world prior to the birth of the dhampir.

"A Medium? A unique choice, to be sure. His father, Varen, didn't have access to any such abilities," the vampire mused. "Maybe it comes from his mother's side? Never the matter. He is still going to die. Correct, Lord Marshal?"

"Correct. We will eradicate the dhampir, along with his ghouls. I even plan to call in those Alda zealots to get the job done."

The marshal had no choice but to respond to this request from the vampire. He didn't crave eternal life, nor feel obliged due to receiving the rank of count. Rather, he required the strength of the vampire for his own plans.

The nation of Thomas's birth, the Milg Shield Kingdom, had belonged to the Amidd Empire since the nation's inception. The royal family of the Milg Shield Kingdom had been reduced to mere counts in the Amidd Empire and forced to defend against constant attacks, while the Empire snatched up all the glory for their victories. During peacetime they were carefully controlled, with any attempts to build their national strength curtailed. If they overcame all that and managed to somehow increase their might, the Empire whittled it down by forcing them into pointless expeditions. One particularly nasty example of this tactic was a giant purge 200 years ago. They lost many of their commanders, great heroes, and a holy lance that had been a national treasure. They had then been forced to offer up all spoils from the excruciating war campaign as tribute, without even getting to expand their territory.

After all of this terrible treatment, it was only natural that the nobles of the Milg Shield Kingdom had come to desire one simple word: independence.

Thomas's plan was to achieve that desire for his nation. Once the Milg Shield Kingdom had become the Milg Kingdom, he would also assume a higher standing. To this end, he needed to gradually increase the strength of the Milg Shield Kingdom, while also gradually weakening the Amidd Empire. Achieving that required the strength of the vampires, who hated the Amidd Empire.

"But you are bringing in the high priest?" the vampire asked. "He is a candidate for the next cardinal. You plan to give him another leg up toward that goal?"

"I also plan to have Raily, the Green Gale Spear, take part," Thomas said.

"Ahaha. The man who left the Five Hue Blades after they departed the Milg Shield Kingdom. A grade C who only got his alias by standing beside Heinz! How much help will he be?"

"He is already grade B. If you are so worried, why don't you join in too? Although it is a three-day, sun-drenched journey to reach the demon barren."

"No need to risk the sunburn," the vampire cackled. "We trust you, human. Now, did you make contact just to provide this report?"

"No, there's something I want to confirm with you," Thomas said. "About the dhampir. That incident in Evbejia when everything turned into golems—was that also the work of this dhampir?"

He was referring to a strange incident that happened more than a year ago, with the walls defending the town, the lord's house, and even the adventurers' guild suddenly turning into golems and walking away.

The magicians' guild was still helping to discover the cause, but it wasn't a case of not yet capturing the culprit—they still didn't even know how it had been done. All they had were suppositions with plenty of holes.

Thomas had since started to suspect that the dhampir was responsible. He hadn't suggested it that morning, in front of Viscount Valchez and Luchiriano, because he lacked conclusive proof, and it still seemed completely insane to him too.

"Don't be preposterous," the vampire replied at once. To the vampire, this suggestion was nothing but a bad joke. "You humans seem to overestimate dhampirs, perhaps due to them having less weaknesses than we full vampires. The abilities of a dhampir, and in particular their vampiric strengths, stem from the parent on the vampire side. If that parent is skilled in magic, then the child likely will be too. If the parent can turn into a bat, then the child likely will also be able to."

"Which also means if the parent vampire lacks magical skill, the child is likely to lack it too," Thomas said. "I know that much."

As the vampire and Thomas had said, a vampire's vampiric abilities depended on the child's vampire parent. It was something of an irony for the evil god faction vampires that a dhampir child, created with blood from another race, should take most strongly after the vampire parent.

"Varen had a powerful resistance to sunlight," the vampire said, "but that aside, he was just a subordinate species who was markedly powerful for his age. I've been told he could only use simple magic. His jobs were Apprentice Thief, Thief, and Fighter. It's unlikely he had any untapped potential. And even if the child had that potential, he could never make use of it at just one or two years of age."

"All true."

"Surely the mother is more suspicious? If the dhampir is a Medium, he must have drawn on power from his mother's spirit."

Those with Medium jobs could converse with spirits to gain knowledge. An advanced Medium could even use the magic that spirits had possessed in life. The vampire was suggesting that the infant Medium had mastered his alchemist mother's techniques from a young age to become a Medium, but this time Thomas shut that down.

"We investigated the mother. She was a grade D adventurer, with some anima magic but no alchemy skills. She couldn't have possessed any abilities of such potency."

"In that case, it must be coincidence. Just two things that happened close together," the vampire said. "Is that all you need? Then I will take my leave. I might have eternal life, but I still need to make good use of my time."

The bat then silently flapped its wings and flew away. Thomas watched it go with a sigh, and then rose and closed the window behind it.

"Coincidence, you say," he muttered.

The incident in Evbejia wasn't just an odd occurrence in some small town out in the sticks. It was a major event that shook the entire nation and was still being investigated to that day. The reason was simple: what if the same thing was to happen, but in a key strategic location? Such an occurrence would render defenses meaningless, no matter the construction of the fortress or the height of the castle walls. Indeed, if the golems acted differently from the Evbejia example, choosing to attack the people inside, the strength of the force garrisoned there wouldn't matter either. All the soldiers there would perish. The walls, ceiling, and floor would literally start attacking them. There was no military formation that could stand against such an incursion.

The only way to prevent that was to understand how the walls had been turned into golems. But even the highest echelons of the magicians' guild had been unable to produce a meaningful answer.

Golems were created by alchemists who took considerable time and magical power to do so. First, they gathered the materials for the golem, then divided them up into sections such as the limbs and body, before using various media, spirit medicines, and magic on each individual part. The process was completed by embedding the golem with an artificial core that allowed it to move. So it was impossible for the town walls, lord's manor, and adventurers' guild building—all completed structures—to turn into golems, let alone the tilled soil.

If there was an alchemist capable of such a feat, it wasn't just the Milg Shield Kingdom—the entire Amidd Empire would do everything it could to bring them under its control. If that wasn't possible, the Empire would put all of its strength to the task of eradicating them.

"It has to be. Has to be a coincidence," Thomas finally muttered. There was no way a three-year-old dhampir could pull off something like that.

Thomas's face returned to the hardened visage of Marshal Palpapekk. He picked up his pen and looked back at the pile of documents.

If Luchiriano had realized that the Ent-wood walls of the orc settlement had been turned into Wood Golems, or noticed the vast reserve of MP that Vandal was working with, Marshal Palpapekk might have made a different decision—even if, at this juncture in time, it was already too late to do anything about it.

It all boiled down to one fundamental mistake: judging something that had never happened before, a child dhampir becoming the king of a bunch of ghouls, by the same yardstick that he had applied to everything else up until that point.

Around the time Marshal Palpapekk was conversing with the vampire, Vandal and the others were heading back to the Ghoul Grotto.

The one hundred or so female ghouls they had rescued had been kept in terrible conditions for a long time, with their food curtailed to keep them weak. Some of them had bones that were broken and then set incorrectly, making it difficult for them to walk long distances. The female adventurers who wanted to undergo the ghoul ceremony had also lost a lot of strength. That left Vandal and his allies with the problem of transporting more than one hundred dilapidated women through the monster-filled demon barrens.

The problem was solved by Sam and some wagons created by Vandal.

"Rise, merge, transform," Vandal commanded.

There were remains of the Ent-wood golems scattered everywhere, fallen where the orcs had destroyed them. Vandal turned them into Wood Golems once again, and then used his Golem Creation skill to merge the remains into a single mass of wood. Then he had used Sam as an example and turned that wood into a couple of carriages.

Normally it would be impossible to create a wagon simply from wood, without any metal at all. It worked in this instance because of two factors. First, because of the Ent-wood lumber, which was as strong as steel while retaining the properties of wood. And second, because every carriage was a golem. They could move on their own, without the need to be pulled.

There were plenty of raw materials lying around. Under Bugogan's orders, the orcs must have almost wiped out the Ents from this demon barren in order to make their mighty walls.

"You could make a fine living in a human town with that trick, boy," Zadilis commented.

"Making carriages? I've got good materials here, but I don't think these would sell very well when put up against something made by an actual carriage craftsman."

"No, I mean the way you handle those materials. In human society, people have to spend money to obtain raw timber, correct? But you can make fresh lumber from a pile of sawdust."

"True. I can work with anything other than burnt-out ashes, I suppose," Vandal said.

Wood wasn't like metal—there was no melting it down and reforging it. That placed a much greater burden on the skills of the carpenter. But Vandal could use his Golem Creation skill to freely return a pile of scraps into a single piece of wood, without any technical woodworking skills. If he wanted to, he could use the branches cut off when processing tree trunks, and even the sawdust created by cutting them off, to make poles or planks of wood. This was so revolutionary that even a ghoul, from a society with no economic culture of its own, took note of it.

"But I'm not really looking for a job," Vandal continued, not sounding especially enamored with the idea.

"Huh? Why not? You could make a fortune."

Vandal gave a sigh. "Because it would be a pain in the ass to make that fortune," he replied.

What Vandal was doing here was basically recycling waste materials to create second-hand wood. On Earth, the concept of recycled wood would surely have taken off, with the drive for sustainability that world had been in the midst of when he died. But in Ramda, they didn't have such heavy industry. Forget complex machines; there weren't even steam engines here. Vandal wasn't sure how much play "environmentally friendly" would get, or if people were even aware of such a concept. So how much would second-hand materials made from trash really be worth?

To top it off, it was only possible due to the Golem Creation skill. Vandal was planning on learning alchemy and starting to make magic items, but even those wouldn't allow other people to copy this particular ability. In other words, Vandal would have to do all the work himself.

Ultimately, making recycled wood using the Golem Creation skill could simply leave him working long hours for pitiful pay. Vandal, struggling with his luxury complex, did not welcome such a choice.

"I might be able to make some money with rare or expensive wood, like ebony on Earth. I should be able to do the same thing with stone, too, so maybe . . . with marble?" Vandal wondered. "Ah, but if there's something like a stonemasons' guild, they might be able to trace the source of the stone . . . and there might be a woodcutters' guild too . . ."

"Human society sounds complex. Boy, don't let one comment from me fry your brain," Zadilis interjected, seeking to bring Vandal back from the ledge as the child clutched at his head.

As it turned out, the Ent wood that Vandal was currently using to make his carriages sold in human society for ten times that of regular wood like cedar or pine, but it would be a while longer before Vandal found that out.

Vandal acquired the skill Carpentry! Enhance Brethren skill level increased!

Young master! Fear not. I can handle this!

Sam had already ranked up from all the experience he

earned during the fight. He had rolled over not only orcs, who were the same rank 3 as his Ghost Carriage had been, but also a rank 5 Orc General, and he had even finished off the rank 7 Noble Orc, Bugogan. All of that provided him with a large chunk of experience.

As a result, the nasty-looking spikes that Talea had outfitted him with had now merged with the wagon itself, and he became a rank 4 Blood Carriage. As a result, he had also acquired two new skills—Size Control and Smooth Handling. These were both going to help him in transporting the compromised women.

Size Control allowed him to change the size of his body, that being the carriage. He could go from his current three-horse size up to a larger four-horse, or down to a smaller two-horse. Smooth Handling, meanwhile, allowed him to maintain the comfort of his passengers regardless of the terrain they were traveling through. The Resist Impact skill he held prior to that already reduced carriage vibrations. He had a dangerous-sounding new name, but he was also becoming more convenient.

Alongside Vigaro and Sam, many of the other ghouls had also ranked up from the experience they had received during the battle, becoming Ghoul Warriors or Ghoul Grapplers. Vandal's own minions, Saria and Rita, and the Skeleton Bird had also ranked up. Saria and Rita had gone from 3 to rank 4, but their races remained unchanged, still Living One-Piece Swimsuit Armor and Living Bikini Armor. That probably meant they still weren't making full use of the abilities of the armor they were inhabiting, but were at least making some progress toward that goal. Their race names hadn't changed because they were growing, but not completely at ease with the armor.

I want to become a higher type of monster as quickly as possible, Rita said, *to prevent you having to put your body on the line again like that, young master! I will become the best maid you've ever seen!*

I know you don't think a monster can be a maid, young master, but Rita and I are serious about this! Saria added.

The two of them had been shocked by the sight of Vandal, bloody and sliced up on the ground. That had renewed their fervor to become stronger. Vandal couldn't complain about such a development.

The Skeleton Bird, meanwhile, had become a rank 4 Specter Bird. The spirit body surrounding its bones now glowed even brighter. From a distance it looked like a sparkly, delightful bird, but some regions apparently considered the arrival of a Specter Bird to be an evil omen. Vandal had to hope that the Olbaum Electorate Kingdom was not one such region.

There was something else they needed to transport a large volume of back to the Ghoul Grotto: the spoils of victory, those being the corpses of their defeated foes.

This issue, however, was resolved very easily. Vandal could have them walk themselves.

After draining the blood from the corpses of the orcs, kobolts, and tamed beasts, and then using Maintain Freshness to prevent any decay, Vandal turned them into zombies. That removed any need for them to be carried by anyone else, although it did create a lot of ambient groaning noise.

As a considerable bonus, the zombies made great pack mules, carrying the weapons and armor they had themselves used in life, along with gear they had stolen from adventurers. With death attribute magic stopping their decay, their flesh and organs were still fresh. Once they returned to the grotto, Vandal could remove the spirits he had placed inside the bodies and turn into more raw ingredients for the cookpot.

Other monsters on the way knew none of this, however, and recognized them as zombies rather than potential prey. The monsters held off from attacking, so there was no need to provide any protection for the zombies. The only disadvantage was their slow movement, but that didn't matter when the weakened ghoul women were also thrown into the mix.

"This so easy!" Vigaro said, clearly impressed. "You do this all prey in future, Vandal!"

Vandal was walking along himself, ignoring the muffled grunting of Bugogan's zombie and feeling better about everything since his discussion with Zadilis.

There was space for him with Sam on one of the other carriages, if he wanted it. But he would soon be turning three, so it was time for him to work harder on building some muscles.

Say, Vandal. Could I become undead or a golem? his mother asked. *Then I could be strong enough to fight alongside you. Wouldn't that be lovely?*

"I like the idea, but I don't think we should risk it. If you inhabit something for too long, it will change the shape of your spirit, and I might not be able to revive you at all."

The spirit of a completely different creature would eventually take on the shape of any host form it was left inside of for too long. For example, Sam was originally a human male, but if his spirit was removed from the carriage that he now inhabited, he probably wouldn't look very much like he had in life, but closer to the carriage he had become. That was how easily the spirit body changed shape after it left a corporeal cage. Maintaining its original shape required powerful determination, hatred, and attachment to the world.

"You have almost no rage or anger, mom, so I think you'd quickly become influenced by whatever I put you inside. It doesn't sound like a good idea to me."

To be quite honest, Vandal couldn't quite believe the state Dalshia was in—that she had almost no hatred, and no desire for revenge. She had been killed in such a brutal fashion that it seemed impossible that she wouldn't be angry or hold any grudges. He had asked her about it once, but she had just said, "I'm fine so long as you are alive and well."

Okay. But if I agree to that, you have to promise not to almost kill yourself again, she replied.

But the fact that the reason his mother didn't hold a grudge was because Vandal was still alive only increased his personal anger toward the perpetrators.

If you have to fight these humans who are coming next, don't do anything too dangerous.

It wasn't time for revenge yet. It wouldn't be that time for a while longer yet. Vandal buried his desire for revenge deep inside.

"Sure, I promise," he said. "I won't do anything too risky."

Name: Skeleton Bird
Rank: 4
Race: Specter Bird
Level: 37
——Passive Skills
[Night Vision] [Spirit Body: Level 3 (UP!)] [Brute Strength: Level 2]
——Active Skills
[Sneaking Steps: Level 1] [High Speed Flight: Level 2

(UP!)] [Fire Missiles: Level 2 (NEW!)]

Name: Sam
Rank: 4
Race: Blood Carriage
Level: 72
——Passive Skills
[Spirit Body: Level 3] [Brute Strength: Level 3] [Off-Road Handling: Level 2]
[Resist Impact: Level 2] [Precision Driving: Level 3] [Comfortable Handling: Level 1 (NEW!)]
——Active Skills
[Sneaking Steps: Level 1] [Speed Driving: Level 1] [Charge: Level 2 (UP!)]
[Size Control: Level 1 (NEW!)]

The Death Mage

CHAPTER FIVE

TRIUMPH, AND DEPARTURE

The ghouls who had remained in the grotto greeted the return of Vandal and the others with cheers.

The ghouls had expanded their village ahead of time. Still, with all the rescued ghouls, they were over capacity again, although no one was especially concerned about that issue at the moment.

The female ghouls and adventurers rested up, while the other started work on processing the food and booty that had walked into the grotto alongside the victorious ghouls. They saved the tongues and eyes of the Kobolt Mages for alchemy ingredients. The pelt of a Kobolt General could be used in armor or clothing, while their fangs could make knives. Normal orcs turned into nothing but meat, but the sinews from an Orc General made excellent bowstrings. The tongue, eyes, and liver of an Orc Mage were useful in alchemy too.

Every part of a Noble Orc had a use. Alongside plenty of meat, the organs could be used for alchemy and potions, the skin for leather, the bones for armor and weapons, the genitals and testicles for strength-boosting elixirs, and that beautiful golden hair—the only "beautiful" thing about the creatures—could be woven into clothing to provide defense against bladed attacks.

Then there were the magic stones. If they could take these to an adventurers' guild, they would fetch a pretty penny.

"Hehehe! Materials, so many materials! What to make first?!" Talea sang happily as she used a knife to butcher the remains of Bugogan.

Vandal looked on, thinking that she looked a bit scary, but also like she was having fun with it.

Then she turned to look directly at him.

"One thing, Lord Van. What are your plans for the future?" She looked psychotic, holding up the bloody knife right next to her face as the fat dripped down. But she was only concerned about what Vandal was going to do next.

A Ghoul King was simply a way to bring multiple grottos together against a common foe. It wasn't an actual race name, like Goblin or Kobolt King. Now that they wiped out the enemies, there was no need for him to remain Ghoul King, or for the ghouls from other grottos to remain in this one. Talea and the others would return to their original homes and go back to life as it had been before he came along.

Which is exactly why I need to take Lord Van back with me! That was Talea's plan.

"About that. There's something I need to talk to you about tomorrow," Vandal replied.

"What?! You want to discuss it with just me? The two of us, alone?" Talea squeaked.

"No. With everyone," Vandal replied.

". . . Ah, yes, of course." She gave a weak laugh.

The ghouls held a feast that evening. They shared skewers of orc meat and orc soup, commemorating their shared struggles in battle. The women who had been prisoners ate particularly ravenously, as though getting some personal revenge on their captors. Even the female adventurers, who had seemed to desire only death, showed improved appetites. Their only wish was to become ghouls and join Vandal's brethren, so Zadilis telling them that they needed to build up some strength to withstand the ceremony was enough to get them eating.

Vandal would never have guessed that his Death Attribute Allure skill would work on humans who lost all will to live.

"If I was on Earth, I'd just have to stand next to a famous suicide spot and I could make a whole bunch of new friends," he muttered. Although that would probably have resulted in him being turned into some kind of object of worship. Even if he had been on Earth, he probably wouldn't have done it.

Vandal chewed on a skewer of Noble Orc. The meat had been roasted with a sauce made from fruit and herbs found in the demon barrens. One nibble was enough to fill his mouth with meaty juices and melting fat, but the sauce prevented any lingering aftertaste. Vandal was pretty sure he could eat as many of these as were available. The overwhelming flavor of the meat almost moved him to tears.

The boar he had eaten after being resurrected in Ramda was delicious, and the Huge Boar meat he ate in this grotto was just as good. But the Noble Orc meat was on another level. Even the highest-quality meat on Earth surely couldn't compare to this. Even Vandal, who had never eaten luxury meat back on Earth, was sure of that.

"I won! I finally beat you at something!" Vandal crowed with victory over his uncle and family, who would never be able to taste this Noble Orc meat on Earth.

To turn human women into ghouls, the ghouls started by digging holes in the ground large enough for the subject to fit inside. Next, they mixed mud with ghoul blood and the toxin from ghoul claws while incanting prayers to the Goddess Vida. They poured this mixture into the holes, submerging the subjects. Three days later, the submerged would turn from humans into ghouls.

"It looks like we're just drowning them," Vandal said. He looked down at the muddy holes containing Kachia and the other women, using magic to detect life down there. He couldn't help himself—normally they would suffocate and die.

"It's fine," Zadilis assured him. "This is the way it's done, although it doesn't work with other monsters or races other than humans. They just choke on mud and die."

"Lord Van, this is how I became a ghoul," Talea said.

Receiving the assurances from the two female elders and still managing to detect life from Kachia and the others, even after ten minutes, finally put Vandal at ease.

"Anyway. What do you want to discuss today?" Zadilis asked.

"Oh, right." The ghouls had gathered, putting their night of victory celebrations behind them. Talea and the others probably believed this was about the handling of the one hundred female ghouls whose grottos had been wiped out, the women who wished to become ghouls, the magic items they had been promised as rewards that would resolve the infertility issues, and what Vandal was planning to do next himself.

Some of the ghoul women had been impregnated by monsters, but a few months after giving birth, they would recover, and each grotto could take around ten. In terms of food, they had just obtained a massive volume that they would literally never be able to eat in time without magical preservation.

The ghouls figured that the female adventurers were to become spoils for Vandal. Then they wouldn't have to bother with explanations after the women became ghouls, and Vandal had proven himself worthy of the prize. There was one ghoul who hadn't undertaken the ritual, and Vandal seemed to be looking after her directly. Everyone assumed she was some kind of favorite of his.

Vandal had promised the magic items as rewards, and Vandal would then either choose one of the grottos or end up with Zadilis and Talea bickering over him. The other ghouls didn't think they were going to have much involvement in this discussion.

But the first thing Vandal said immediately betrayed all expectations.

"Everyone, I need you to listen carefully. By summer, at the very latest, a massive human army is going to be coming here to kill us all."

April. Approximately two months after they received word that the Noble Orcs had been wiped out by the ghouls and their dhampir leader, a force of close to 1,000 humans—led by Marshal Palpapekk himself—entered the jungle demon barren.

They had 300 grade D adventurers, and 200 grade C. Then there was a unit of Divine Alda warriors, led by High Priest Goldan himself, the grade B adventurer Raily, the Green Gale Spear formerly of the Five Hue Blades, plus soldiers and knights.

The marshal had wanted to really drive the point home by also hiring some grade B adventurers, but pulling too many of those together in a single place could have repercussions for defending against monsters in other locations, so he had settled for as many of the better grade C ones as possible.

"Sorry to say it, but that dhampir is mine," Raily cackled with a grin on his face. "Heinz is the reason the dhampir got away once before, but now I'm calling my own shots. Time to really make a name for myself."

"Then so be it!" replied High Priest Goldan with a crooked smirk. "If it means the end of the bloodline of that evil vampire and his elf-witch, then I care not whose hand performs the deed. Our lord above will bless us regardless!"

Raily and the high priest formed the core of the army's fighting strength and were being counted on to deal with any high-ranking ghouls, as well as the dhampir himself. The other adventurers and the knights were to follow their orders.

Both Raily and Goldan were prime examples of adventurers that had physical strength in particular that was likely higher than grade B, edging beyond human limits. This kind of treatment of them was only natural in a party that didn't include any grade A adventurers or above. The scouts Marshal Palpapekk had placed between the town and the demon barrens had kept a close watch to ensure no ghouls left the barrens to attack the town. There had been no such movements.

"The ghouls are lying in wait for us, surely," Goldan said. "I pray that you will not be caught unawares and end up merely as more experience for them."

The ghouls knew the humans were coming, but they hadn't left the demon barren. That meant they had been building their strength and preparing to retaliate once the humans arrived. This was the common perception among all the army leaders, including Goldan Bohmak. For that reason, everyone had tense looks on their faces as they proceeded through the demon barren in question.

"Hey, I know what's going down," Raily replied. "I'm here to finally surpass soft little Heinz, and these ghouls are the steppingstone to do it."

Since leaving the Five Hue Blades, Raily found that his number of designated quests decreased, and his treatment by the guild had also gotten worse. An offer that had come from the marshal himself was a chance to prove himself worthy of more attention, and so it wasn't tension but excitement that covered his face.

His head was full of thoughts of worldly advancement. Marshal Palpapekk definitely had his eye on him, and if he could serve up the head of this dhampir, the marshal's trust would only further increase. He might even be able to take on the responsibility of training the count's knights.

The army entered the demon barrens and began the search for their target. They knew where the Noble Orc settlement was located, but they didn't know the location of the Ghoul Grotto that had spawned the ghouls responsible. The demon barrens were too dangerous to send in scouts, who were excellent for recon but much poorer when it came to combat, and it hadn't seemed worth risking sending adventurers.

This was because they presumed the dhampir was a Medium. A Medium could talk with the spirits of the dead and obtain information from them. So if their scouts or adventurers were discovered by the dhampir, the ghouls could kill them and extract information from their spirits. There was no accounting for the damage a few words from the loose lips of a dead man could cause.

The search, however, was not going well.

"We're only finding goblins and kobolts," a scout complained. "One or two orcs, nothing more. We're yet to see a single ghoul."

"Tell me about it. There are beast-type monsters too, like Huge Boar, Mad Boar, Impaler Bull, Iron Turtle, and Giant Rat . . . but not much else."

The soldiers had expected to at least encounter some smaller units of ghouls, maybe coming to check them out, but they were having trouble finding anything ghoul-related at all.

When they eventually did find a grotto—

"It's no good. Nothing here but some goblins that seem to have taken the place over."

The settlement certainly looked like a ghoul grotto, but there was nothing to see.

"The ghouls are gathered in one spot, waiting to ambush us!" a soldier suggested. "This is bad! Even with our numbers, if they all attack at once . . ."

"I don't care about their numbers!" another shouted. "I'm going to avenge Rikken! Avenge my brother!" He was the older brother of one of the adventurers presumed to have been killed by the orcs. No one had the heart to point out that it was ghouls they were here to kill.

"The women might still be alive."

"Most likely turned into ghouls. All we can do for them now is save their souls, as quickly as possible."

The first adventurer accepted this comment from one of the Alda devout. Death clearly seemed like the best choice for women who had been orc playthings for months prior to being turned into ghouls.

The army made camp on the site of the orc settlement and continued their search from there. However, they continued to encounter anything but ghouls, and even as the days passed, there was no sign of the ghouls coming to attack them.

Of course, they were still spending time in a dangerous demon barren, but they had a combined strength that none of the monsters normally found here could hope to match, so the army started to relax.

"More wagon tracks. What does this mean?"

"That we passed here before?"

"You moron! We left the wagons in the camp!"

The army had brought multiple wagons along in order to carry their provisions. This demon barren was like a jungle, but there were fifteen-foot-long Mad Boars rampaging around it too, carving out paths wide enough for wagons. However, currently the wagons were either left in the camp, or on their way out of the demon barrens to bring in fresh supplies from the town. There was no way these tracks—heading in a completely different direction from the town or the camp—had been made by their own wagons.

"So what are these ruts? Do they look like monster tracks to you?"

"Some adventurers probably passed this way once. There's no hoof prints. Look. The rain washed away everything other than the deepest ruts."

This explanation proved enough for the soldiers and adventurers who noticed them, and the tracks were never reported to anyone higher in the army.

Parties of adventurers often brought wagons into demon barrens to carry out their spoils. Killing orcs and Huge Boars provided large volumes of meat, while chopping down Ents provided valuable wood, but carrying all of this baggage back to civilization demanded a wagon. There were space attribute mages who could place objects in null space and transport them around, and item boxes created by that same kind of mage, but both were rarely available.

These ruts had to be left by adventurers working with more primitive means, the army grunts concluded.

It took two weeks for the army to discover that was wrong. It was then that Marshal Palpapekk and Viscount Valchez started to panic, as the tension of the army relaxed altogether.

"There were wagon tracks that led out of the demon barren? Why didn't we notice this before?!" Goldan shouted at the men who finally made the report.

"The wagon tracks were leading the opposite direction from the town, toward the mountains, so we didn't think anything of them. A vampire, maybe, but no one considered ghouls might be using wagons . . ."

In principle, monsters like goblins and kobolts didn't use wagons. Indeed, they couldn't. They didn't have the skills to make them. Monsters like vampires, who lived in the shadows of human society and lured in humans to act as their minions, had many means to obtain carriages. Goblins and orcs could only get them by stealing. However, roughshod use, no maintenance, and gobbling up the livestock that might pull them meant such wagons soon ended up broken and discarded, or used as material for houses.

Ghouls were far smarter than goblins and orcs, but the adventurers had assumed a similar situation. The more experience adventurers had, the less likely they were to believe that ghouls were riding around in carriages. The soldiers and knights had been told by their commanders to follow the lead of the adventurers, so they had gone along with that.

Now, however, after all this searching, they still hadn't turned up a single ghoul. This reality, coupled with deep tracks leaving the demon barrens, as though dozens of carriages passed the same spot, led to one final conclusion.

"The dhampir has taken the ghouls and fled by carriage?!" Raily roared. "Why didn't anyone notice? Were our scouts asleep?!"

But everyone knew the answer, including him. The scouts had only been watching one area: that between the demon barren and the town. Marshal Palpapekk had never considered that they might run in completely the opposite direction, toward the borderland mountains in the east. Scouts were a limited resource, and so they had all been placed in the west, between the town and the demon barren.

"I can't believe hundreds of ghouls and the dhampir leading them would just run away without fighting! We've been set up!"

High Priest Goldan's embittered cries of rage marked the end of the army's expedition.

Everyone apart from High Priest Goldan—and Raily, who missed out on a chance to make a name for himself—returned to town in high spirits. For them, everything had worked out quite nicely.

They had missed out on the rewards and fame that would have come from taking down the ghouls, but the adventurers had collected a volume of materials, magic stones, and bounty parts by defeating the non-ghoul monsters available for slaying. All their expenses during the expedition were covered by the state, so they hadn't really suffered any losses.

For the knights and soldiers, their time in the army paid a better daily stipend and additional hazard pay, and the ordinary soldiers in particular had gotten to eat rare treats like Mad Boar, so they were happy with the outcome that didn't involve fighting ghouls. Viscount Valchez could have danced a jig—he certainly was inside—at the outcome, what with the ghouls running away over the mountains while the army suffered zero fatalities. Losing knights and soldiers would mean paying compensation to their families, and then finding and training replacements.

He was a little uneasy about failing to wipe the ghouls out, leaving them as a lingering threat. Beyond the mountains, however, lay sprawling demon barrens that could have swallowed his entire domain whole, and Noble Orcs were the least of the concerns out there. There were said to be designated natural-disaster-class dragons out there, lingering on since the age of the gods. Adding a few hundred ghouls to that wasn't going to change anything.

Viscount Valchez was far more interested in the jungle demon barren, the monsters inside of which had just been laid waste by an army of 1,000. Now that the major threats had been removed, if he could have the remaining monsters hunted down and employ magicians to purify the corrupted magical power, there was a chance that he could transform the demon barrens into rich new territory. With that in mind, he didn't have the brain cells to waste on ghouls and dhampirs.

"I can't believe they would run away . . ." Marshal Palpa-pekk sounded like he was chewing a mouthful of bitter bugs.

He proceeded to dispatch some scouts in order to confirm that the ghouls had indeed run into the mountains, and then turned his attention to the next issue: the political ramifications of all this.

The state bursar was going to have a field day, asking if such a budget had been required after they failed to capture the ghouls, and whether he had simply been using it as an excuse to help the viscount purify the demon barrens. Viscount Valchez was the one who benefited the most from this, with the economic potential of such increased territory.

In regard to the dhampir Vandal, the adventurer who had originally identified him had slipped quietly away and the hunt for the child ended with nothing. The name "Vandal" was not included in any reports pertaining to the operation and remained nothing but conjecture in the heads of a few of those involved.

The day after the victory against the orcs, Vandal had let the ghouls know the humans were coming. Their response, of course, was to stand and fight.

"We strong now! We fight hundreds humans easily!" Vigaro proclaimed, a fist raised into the air, and many of the ghouls agreed. They had leveled up from the fight with the orcs, with many of them ranking up too. It was true. The ghouls were now far stronger than they had been before. But still . . .

"I'm sorry, Vigaro. We can't win." Vandal shot down the idea.

"Why?"

"King, we strong! We not lose to humans!"

"We win with you! Why you say different?"

"Fight with us!"

Faced with the barrage of badly articulated words from various ghouls, Vandal picked his words carefully.

"Yes, we are stronger," he said. "If the same number of humans as us came, we would win. But unlike the orcs, the humans are going to prepare for us. This time, we'll be the ones under attack."

They wouldn't be able to raid the humans, like they did with the orcs. The humans would come in large numbers, with powerful warriors.

"And they will keep coming, over and over, until we are defeated. If we defeat the first raid, they will send another, and if we defeat that, another. They will keep coming and coming."

Even if they defeated the first army to come, the Milg Shield Kingdom would be unable to leave such dangerous monsters unchecked, and obviously send a second force.

If this was a fight between humans, they would find a way to settle, or work to end the fighting. But for humans, ghouls were just monsters. Furthermore, the demon barren was only three days from a town. They weren't going to compromise here.

The only way to stop them would be to do something about the entire Milg Shield Kingdom itself—indeed, the Amidd Empire, which would surely get involved before the Milg Shield Kingdom exhausted itself. That was simply not in the realm of what Vandal and his allies could accomplish.

"The boy is right," Zadilis said. "The humans were already gathering a force to take down the Noble Orcs. They must have numerous adventurers and knights who could defeat the boy or the Noble Orc."

That silenced Vigaro. The ghouls grumbled and moaned.

Zadilis had a pained expression on her own face, however. They had only just finished dealing with the Noble Orcs, after all. To make it worse, the ghouls weren't even planning on attacking the human settlement. All they wanted was to keep on living here in the demon barrens like before. But the humans would still consider them a danger and send troops to wipe them out. From the ghouls' perspective, it was extremely unfair.

While it didn't show on Vandal's face, this was hard on him too. He considered Zadilis and the others his family, and he had failed to deliver them what they wanted. To protect this place, he would've needed to erect a series of stoic fortresses, surround the entire demon barren in a stone wall, and create an army of thousands of golems.

"We also have other people we need to protect," Vandal said. Most of the women they had just saved were pregnant and incapable of fighting. There were also other pregnant ghouls, like Bildy. No one wanted to put them in danger.

Talea sighed and spoke up. "We wish for the continuation of our race. Rather than a victory for just a handful of us, we should choose a defeat that allows as many of us as possible to survive."

At these words, the ghouls mostly lost their will to fight. Those that still wanted to were talked down by Zadilis, silenced by Vigaro, and persuaded by Talea. Ghouls lived in a world of survival of the fittest, so those without the power to change it could only accept this outcome.

"But what are we going to do?" Basdia asked. "We can't hide, but we can't run either."

The ghouls needed the demon barrens. If they left, their ability to reproduce would only further decrease, not to mention it would be more difficult to find food. They couldn't suddenly become farmers.

"I have an idea where we can run to," Vandal said. "It's a bit of a distance away." He explained about the bug undead that he sent out scouting, as a backup in case they failed to defeat the Noble Orc, and the demon barrens the bugs had discovered. That resolved the biggest issue—a destination.

This destination was the demon barren located beyond the mountains to the east. He couldn't see many details through the limited eyes of the bugs, but the area appeared to be the ruins of a large city. More than enough room for all the ghouls.

Even better, the bugs told him there were other undead in this demon barren. Vandal's Death Attribute Allure could turn undead into more allies.

That settled matters. The ghouls immediately started planning their relocation.

W*rooooooooooooagh!*

It was the howling of Ents. The ghouls started by chopping down enough Ents to almost wipe them out. Vandal turned the wood they collected into a fleet of Cursed Carriages.

Looks like I've got to set a good example, Sam quipped.

Vandal made the spirits of the dead orcs occupy the carriages, so they didn't have skills like Precision Driving, but sturdy carriages that could move on their own were enough for the moment.

Once the female adventurers had completed the process of becoming ghouls, they boarded the carriages, still unsteady in their own bodies, along with the other pregnant ghouls. Then the caravan set out from the demon barren. Vandal had already used Lemures and bug undead to confirm there were no enemy scouts on the mountainside, and so it was a leisurely departure.

It was April, more than a month after leaving the jungle demon barren. Vandal was sitting in Sam's wagon, leading the ghoul group. The route was harsh, but the trip was going smoothly—apart from three issues.

"Crossing these mountains is easier than expected," Zadilis said.

"Thanks to the furs," Vandal said.

They had used furs from monsters in the jungle demon barrens to make the protective gear required to cross the high-altitude mountains. The ghouls were much tougher than humans, so they didn't suffer from things like altitude sickness either. They were a little more lethargic than usual, if that was possible, due to having left the demon barrens behind, but Enhance Brethren helped to cover that gap. A mountain climber on Earth would question the quality of their gear, but this wasn't Earth, and they weren't humans.

The issue wasn't their equipment or supplies, but the route itself. There were frequent slopes that a skilled mountain climber would struggle with, let alone carriages filled with people.

"Boy, we need a road again," Zadilis said.

"All right."

The slopes were not a problem, ultimately, as long as Vandal didn't run out of MP. After turning the mountain surface into golems, he used Golem Creation to create a path that the carriages could traverse. He carved out the mountainside to make narrow paths wider and dug tunnels through steep cliffs.

Vandal had first considered using Golem Creation and brute magical power—business as usual—to simply carve a path directly beneath the mountains, but that plan had been nixed because of the dangers of cave-ins as well as the risk of hitting an underground water source.

After the carriages passed through, Vandal let the path return to narrow, inhospitable mountainside. Vandal had been worried that the Milg Shield Kingdom might send scouts after them and was cleaning up—or messing up—behind them, just in case. That proved to be the right move, because when the scouts that Marshal Palpapekk had sent out a month behind Vandal and the others reached the foot of the mountains, they had quickly decided further pursuit was impossible and turned back.

Which left them only three problems: monsters, medical care, and the baby boom.

These mountains were known as the Boundary Mountains. That wasn't the boundary between the Amidd Empire and the Olbaum Electorate Kingdom, but rather the boundary between the human and monster worlds. As the name suggested, they were almost completely unexplored and covered with demon barrens—which in turn meant monsters would attack a party of this scale moving through them.

However, as Vandal laid their path to weave between these demon barrens, the monsters that attacked them were those living on the fringes. The weak monsters, at least for the region.

"I defeated wolf that look like hedgehog!" Vigaro shouted.

"I've never seen that monster before," Basdia said. "I wonder if it tastes good?"

"Looks good, looks good."

To top it off, the monsters had low intelligence, not smart

enough to understand the danger of attacking hundreds of ghouls. Fighting them off provided fresh meat and furs for more warm clothing. They had started to run low on orc meat already, so this was actually a big help.

That said, sometimes bigger beasts attacked.

"A flock of wyverns!"

On that day, wyverns attacked them from above. These were the lowest ranking of dragon-type monsters, with wings for front legs and not especially smart. There was some debate among scholars about whether they should be called dragons at all.

They didn't breathe fire or use magic, but they were still rank 5 monsters with excellent flight capabilities, and sharp teeth and claws that were as powerful as they looked. Taking out their wings dropped them down a rank, comparatively speaking, but the battle took place in the mountains, probably 6000 feet above sea level. The wyverns had the advantage.

And while the wyverns weren't smart, they were also smarter than animals, gathering their allies prior to the attack and targeting locations where the ghouls' defenses were weakest, such as the rear of the train.

This time there were five enemies. That wasn't an easy number to deal with.

"Gaaah!"

The ghouls gave a signal using their battle language. The warriors unleashed a rain of arrows while the women used attack spells. But the ghouls had lived in a jungle with prey happy to close in with them, so their ranged prowess was comparatively limited. Plenty of ghouls had the Bow Proficiency skill, including Basdia, but none of them had it particularly high.

Caw, caw!

Gaaoooooo!

In these kinds of situations, Vandal could rely on the Skeleton Bird, which had reached a rank 4 Specter Bird. Vandal's Enhance Brethren skill further strengthened it, meaning even wyverns had to take notice.

Two of the winged terrors instinctually peeled off to confront the Skeleton Bird. They clearly believed that two of them would deal with the problem more easily. It wasn't a bad plan, coming from these wyverns, because the Skeleton Bird's biggest asset was its mobility.

However . . .

Shaaaaaa! Distracted by their prey and the Skeleton Birds, the invisible Lemures had moved into position, and then they popped out with a terrible intent to kill.

The wyverns screeched in terror, swerving toward this new threat, their tiny brains in chaos. Three of them immediately gave up and fled, while the remaining two were significantly slowed down.

"Two left!"

"Meeeeat!"

Arrows and magic rained down on the dulled wyverns. With their mobility stripped away, they were little better than sitting ducks, and their scales weren't hard enough to protect against Brute Strength-powered arrows and magical attacks. The remaining wyverns decided to flee, but that only exposed them further. Skeleton Bird unleashed spirit body missiles, then dug boney claws into their exposed necks.

The third wyvern crashed into the mountainside, leaving two alive. They sped up their escape. Vandal reached out toward them for a moment, but then lowered his arm without doing anything.

"You need to conserve your MP, Van. Using the Lemures was enough," Basdia said.

This whole trip will fall apart if we lose you, young master, Sam said. *Take care of yourself.*

"I'm aware," Vandal replied. He had been thinking of seeing if death attribute magic could reduce their lift, but Vandal was needed to make the road. They would be stopped in their tracks if Vandal collapsed, not to mention exposed to dangers like rockslides.

Vandal had to pay much closer attention to his MP than normal until they finished crossing the mountains. In the face of raw nature, one hundred million, ten billion, no amount of magical power could ever be enough.

A young ghoul poked her head out of one of the wagons. "That's plenty of meat too."

She was right. Three wyverns would feed the ghouls well for today. They might have been low ranking, but they were still dragons, making them delicious and nutritious. Their organs could be used in alchemy, but also provided energy if eaten. The ghouls could use their scales, bones, and hides for armor, and their fans and claws for weapons.

"Defeating three of them, wow," Kachia said. "If you could get these to the adventurers' guild, then we'd be set for at least a little while."

"Think you could deliver them?" Vandal asked her.

"Nope. Not even one," she replied.

Kachia, now a ghoul, had been the female adventurer Bubobio had laid claim to. Noble Orcs were powerful individuals but not prolific when it came to breeding power, luckily, and so Kachia had not become pregnant. She had been saved by Basdia and the others, and then undergone the ritual to become a ghoul.

"The guild will be treating us as killed in action, and women who have been defiled by monsters are not well treated. Becoming a ghoul was the best choice. It's not like I have any family."

She had been close to a mental breakdown at first, but had now recovered enough to have a more philosophical perspective. She was still pretty frightened of men, however, which was why she was riding in Sam's wagon: Vandal was a child and Sam was undead.

They stopped to butcher the wyverns, while Vandal kept Skeleton Bird and some Lemures watching the skies. This kind of attack tended to happen at least once a day, indicating how hard it was to make the mountain crossing. Regular adventurers would have tapped out in days. Vandal wouldn't have made it much longer himself, without his massive magical power and his Resist Maladies skill to ward off altitude sickness.

At least monster attacks allowed them to replenish their supplies. The other two problems were more difficult to deal with.

The sound of crying infants now rose into the air. A Black Goblin baby had tried to climb down from the halted wagons, taking a tumble and starting to cry. That had surprised a black kobolt baby, so he started crying too.

"Hey, little one! You can't leave the wagon."

"What is it? Are you hungry? You sure do drink a lot," said another.

Two female ghouls picked up the babies and started to feed them. Yes, these were the parents of the baby monsters.

Many of the ghoul women they had rescued from the Noble Orc settlement had been pregnant. That was the reason they had been taken captive, so it was an unavoidable result. Vandal had explained that he could use his death attribute magic to limit damage to their bodies while terminating the fetuses, but they rejected that proposal.

"If we care for them from the moment of their birth, they will follow us," Zadilis had said.

So that was how it worked. They wouldn't use their wombs to obtain goblin or orc children in times of peace, but in emergency situations, they could keep the pregnancies to make up for lost numbers. The grotto the female ghouls had come from had lost all of their males, and so they were probably looking to bolster their strength.

As it turned out, all the goblin, kobolt, and orc children who were born had black skin and hair. Goblins were normally green-skinned, and orcs a pale pink. Kobolts sometimes had black fur, but being completely black for them was rare.

The cause, most likely, was Vandal's magical power. Vandal hadn't wanted departing the demon barrens to have a negative effect on the children, so Vandal gave the fetuses a bolstering shot of Magical Power Transfer in order to keep them in the same condition as in the demon barrens. That had allowed the fetuses to grow at the same rate as when in the barrens and be born alive and well—and also black. There was nothing wrong with that, and he wasn't going to call it some bad omen. He checked them out with Appraisal, and sure enough . . .

Black Goblin Baby.

Anubis Baby.

Orcas Baby.

Those were the names for the goblin, kobolt, and orc babies. Somehow, new breeds.

"What does this all mean? Got any ideas for me, Darwin?" Vandal muttered.

"Who's that, Van?" Basdia asked. "One of the horrible scientists from the world called Origin?"

"No. Someone older and important, from a different world," Vandal said. He looked up into the sky for a moment, having seemingly created some new breed of monsters, but he was asking the wrong person.

"It doesn't seem like a problem to me," Zadilis said. "They look smarter than normal goblins, stronger than normal kobolts, and larger than normal orcs."

"Nothing to worry," Vigaro added. "Females have babies, males raise them up. Same for me."

"Me too. Vigaro raised me up good," Basdia said.

No one seemed to think the situation was anything to worry about. Not that it was a problem Vandal could do anything about, even if he did worry. He had already given magical power to all the pregnant women.

This takes me back, Dalshia said. *I fed you just like that, Vandal. You weren't all that eager to start with, but you soon latched right on there . . .*

"Hey, what's going on? Why is Vandal shivering?" Kachia asked.

He's fine, Rita said. *Lady Dalshia was just remembering when she used to breastfeed him, and it was giving the young master an uncomfortable flashback.*

You're still a child, young master, Saria consoled him. *You've got nothing to be embarrassed about. Have some confidence!*

Kachia was clearly surprised at Vandal's sudden strange reaction, but for the sisters who could see Dalshia, it was just another day at the races. Even Zadilis and the other ghouls, who also couldn't see Dalshia, were no longer surprised by Vandal suddenly wigging out.

The real issue with the baby boom, anyway, was that it kept reminding Vandal of his own infantile experiences!

Fortunately for the overstimulated Vandal, the baby boom didn't last very long. The reproductive power of monsters was not to be underestimated, and soon the captured ghoul females had all given birth. It would only take a month from there for the rapidly growing monster babies to leave breastfeeding behind.

"Vandal, if my baby is a boy, can I really name him after you?" Bildy asked, her own tummy swollen with seven months of pregnancy. "You have a fine, strong, ghoul-sounding name."

They were still waiting for the ten ghoul females whom Vandal had helped conceive to give birth. Unlike the other monsters, ghouls also grew up at a similar pace to humans.

"This is going to keep happening if I fix the infertility problem, huh," Vandal muttered. The spirit Dalshia had a fractured memory, meaning the same triggers made her repeat the same information over and over. Vandal's eyes glazed over as he realized he was going to still be hearing the phrase "latched on" a lot in his future.

The final problem they faced was caring for the ghouls suffering from physical issues after leaving the demon barrens. All care was being taken to ensure they didn't become seriously sick. Talea fell especially ill.

"Ah, how can I ever make up for this, Lord Van?" Talea moaned. She looked so old and frail that Vandal was constantly tempted to quip that he doubted she ever would. She had been full of energy—too much energy—back in the demon barrens, and fully behind the idea of moving, but leaving had weakened her substantially in both body and mind.

"You are pathetic," Zadilis said. "Show some spine, girl."

"You should be older than me!" Talea griped. "How are you so full of energy?"

Talea's advanced age did seem to be the cause. Zadilis, meanwhile, had been rejuvenated by Vandal back down to the actual physical age her body appeared to be. The fact that ghouls stopped aging prevented anyone from noticing.

"Just when"—Talea broke off for a fit of coughing—"I finally obtained some wyvern materials. I hardly ever got to use those when I was human."

"Once we reach the new demon barren, you'll be up and making new gear in no time," Vandal assured her.

But even as he spoke, he furtively checked her for any signs of encroaching demise. If it came down to it, then he would use Rejuvenation on her too. It might stir up some funny rumors again, but that would be worth keeping her alive.

"Thank you, Lord Van. But please, look after her as well." Talea pointed at the Living Dead lying next to her.

After being abandoned by Luchiriano, it really had become a living corpse, doing nothing but breathing, so it needed to be attended to in all other ways. Living Dead counted as undead from the perspective of having no soul, but their bodies were alive. They would starve without food, get sick if they weren't kept clean, and get bedsores if left lying down all day. Even without a soul, it was hard for others to watch someone go through all that, and it could negatively impact the fetus that was growing inside the Living Dead.

The fetus was still there, the result of Noble Orc Bugogan impregnating the Living Dead and then Vandal removing the monster elements from it and placing the soul of the original mother inside of it. It was only around two months since the body became pregnant, but the bump was already showing. That had to be whatever Noble Orc influence remained.

"Preparing the wyverns will take a while anyway," Talea said.

Vandal scooped up the Living Dead and carried it over next to Talea, cot and all. Kachia was surprised again at the strength his slender arms displayed, thanks to his Brute Strength skill. He was already stronger than the average adult male, so there was no point in using magic for this task. He was surrounded by ghouls with their own Brute Strength and other undead, so the only one surprised by any of this was Kachia, who had still been a human just two months ago.

"What shall we talk about today?" Vandal asked, oblivious to Kachia's surprise. "I know—what to do when you arrive at our destination." He was talking to the Living Dead—or more precisely, to the fetus inside her.

He had seen on TV on Earth that talking to a fetus was good for its development. It was a foreign documentary about how geniuses were born. On Earth, Vandal's father had kept him completely away from all forms of luxury but had been strangely forgiving toward anything that he didn't consider luxurious. That meant Vandal had been able to watch TV—if not all the time—and also use the Internet. Of course, what Vandal's uncle considered "luxury" had changed from day to day, meaning he needed to keep his guard up. Vandal certainly didn't feel any gratitude.

Vandal started to talk about how they could rebuild the ruins in the demon barrens, hunt delicious monsters, fix up a public bath—if they could find one—and take a relaxing bath, and also finally ferment some walnuts and acorns to make a miso-like paste. He painted the picture of a bright and cheerful future, even without resolving his grudges from his previous life. He talked so much that his knowledge from his previous lives started to leak out, with Kachia asking in puzzlement about "miso." But Vandal didn't notice that either.

"We're almost like one big family," Talea said with a weak smile.

". . . You'll have to explain that family tree," Kachia replied sarcastically.

At a glance, while the three were clearly different races, the three of them might look like a pregnant mother—the Living Dead—being watched over by a daughter, Talea, and her younger brother, Vandal.

"Talea, you minx! Becoming family with Van before me!" Bildy complained.

"Hahaha, nothing for you to worry about!" Zadilis cackled. "She probably feels more like his grandmother!"

"Hey, I can hear you! Oh, Lord Van! Zadilis is thirty years older than me! Don't let the old bat mock me like this!"

"Yes, yes, we're all one big happy family," Vandal said placatingly.

And so, thanks to Vandal's command of his magical power, the trip across the mountains proceeded, at least as smoothly as could be expected.

Acquired Engineering skill!

After passing the midpoint in May—around the time the people of Japan would be coming down from their Golden Week national holiday high—Vandal and his party finally crossed the mountains and reached their destination, the ruins demon barren.

The area was located in a basin between the mountain ranges and took three days to cross. The first area Vandal and his party came to must have been fields in the past.

"It took about three months to get here. To get to the Olbaum Electorate Kingdom, there are more mountains to cross, which could take another three months. Even if the Milg Shield Kingdom didn't send their forces after us, it might have taken a year to complete that trip," Vandal mused.

"If it was just you, Vandal, with Sam and the undead, I think you would have been faster," Zadilis reasoned.

Vandal would soon be turning three years old, and he gave a sigh at how far away the Olbaum Electorate Kingdom still felt.

He had other things to do first, anyway, and so he gathered his resolve. They had to head into the ruined demon barren and work together to turn it into a place the ghouls could live. As Vandal looked up at their new base of operations, he found it wreathed in the kind of chilling atmosphere that would send newbie adventurers running for the hills with just a glance.

The high and mighty stone castle walls were cracked and broken in places, with the exposed openings invaded by trees. Beyond the walls sat the ruins of a former town, laid waste before the elements. The white castle itself, which still reared up into the sky, looked like the bony corpse of some skeletal creature.

Even more chilling than all of that, however, was the heavy presence that hung over the abandoned ruins. There was no breeze, and yet the leaves rustled. Strange cries rang out. The thought that it might not be animals making these noises was enough to send shivers down the spine.

It was plain that the ruined demon barren would be home to monsters that even Zadilis and Dalshia had never seen before. Some of them might even be high ranking. Vandal had confirmed the presence of a lot of undead, but that probably wasn't all. There could be a dragon or two making their nest here, or a dangerous dungeon spitting out who knows what.

Vandal would have to build a settlement and find sources of food and raw materials to help the ghouls settle here.

He was still using the bug undead as scouts, but there was a lot he saw through insect eyes that he just couldn't really make out, and some of the bugs had gotten suddenly squished without explanation, probably by monsters. Now he was going to have to face this dangerous and unknown land with his own eyes and ears.

"Kinda exciting."

Vandal wasn't scared of adventuring into the unknown. In fact, the prospect was getting him pumped up. He had lived constricted, narrow lives on Earth and Origin, so coming to new and unexplored places was becoming a source of fun for him. He didn't like the fact that they had arrived here by fleeing from their enemies, but that didn't diminish the vista now spreading before him.

"Okay. We'll spend the night sleeping rough again, keeping some distance from the ruins for now," Vandal said.

"Everyone! Prepare the camp!"

The ghouls quickly took up his orders.

"Get some scouts on watch! We're close to a demon barren, so keep your guard up!"

Vandal's party started to set up camp. The very reason that they didn't know what lay ahead was why they needed to be in top shape, physically and in terms of MP. Now past the baby boom, they had around 600 in the group. Orcs were generally born one at a time, but goblins and kobolts tended to come in threes, and that was the same regardless of the race of the mother. They now had around fifty Black Goblins, one hundred Anubis, and sixty Orcas. Their overall number was already creeping up on that of Bugogan's own settlement.

"King, teach me stuff."

"King, king, I found a cool bone! For you!"

"Huh? King, you shrunk?"

The kids had all taken a liking to Vandal too. Perhaps it was because of the death attribute magic they received in the womb, or maybe they were just following their parents' example. Vandal was happy to be liked, of course, but still.

He took a moment to look up at one of the Orcas, already bigger than him in just two months since being born, and sighed. Vandal was starting to suspect he might not be able to pull off being a noble and a ghoul king at the same time.

Name: Vandal
Race: Dhampir (Dark Elf)
Age: 2 years 11 months
Alias: Ghoul King
Job: None
Level: 100
Job History: None
——Status
Vitality: 48
Magical Power: 113807904
Strength: 42
Agility: 17
Muscle: 47
Intellect: 89
——Passive Skills
[Brute Strength: Level 1] [Rapid Healing: Level 2] [Death Attribute Magic: Level 3]

[Resist Maladies: Level 4] [Resist Magic: Level 1] [Night Vision] [Spirit Pollution: Level 10]

[Death Attribute Allure: Level 3] [Skip Incantation: Level 1] [Enhance Brethren: Level 4 (UP!)]
——Active Skills
[Suck Blood: Level 3] [Limit Break: Level 3] [Golem Creation: Level 3]

[Non-Attribute Magic: Level 1] [Magic Control: Level 1] [Spirit Body: Level 1]

[Carpentry: Level 1 (NEW!)] [Engineering: Level 1

(NEW!)]

——Curses

[Unable to carry over experience from previous lives] [Unable to enter existing jobs] [Unable to personally acquire experience]

The End

The Death Mage

Bonus Chapter
The First and Last Great Ent Hunt

Maybe woodcutters had early mornings.

"Basdia, the sun is setting. Let's set up camp," a ghoul suggested.

"We slept plenty in the daytime. We can rest once the sun comes up," Basdia replied.

Unlike those woodcutters, Basdia and her crew were proceeding through the demon barren regardless of day or night. The ghouls were searching for trees to chop down.

Are you hungry? I'm still bursting with energy, Rita said.

Perhaps the young ghoul didn't have the energy to quip back that the living armor didn't have a stomach to begin with, instead looking around.

"Not much luck so far. Even those we do find are saplings no taller than me," Basdia pondered.

She sounded disappointed, and the group moved on—leaving behind a number of large, tall, round trees. Massive trees that could have made fine pillars or planks. But Basdia and her crew didn't give them a second glance.

"Hey. That one."

Now she did see something, a medium-sized tree that wasn't as tall or thick as the ones they had just left behind. She took a pebble out from the bag at her waist and threw it at the tree.

With the pebble suddenly bouncing off its bark, the tree proceeded to flail its branches around, its roots writhing like feet.

"An Ent! Weapons up, chop it down!" Basdia shouted.

Attack lower than the waist, Rita called.

Neither of them were shaken by the threatening behavior of the Ent, and they raised their weapons and launched a raging attack. This was what they were here for. Tree monsters. Ents.

The ghouls decided they would depart the jungle demon barren and head to new pastures across the eastern mountains. This epic journey would require a fleet of carriages, and the materials for those required the hard-as-steel Ent wood.

The wood recovered from the remains of Bugogan's settlement had not been enough. Basdia and Vigaro therefore split up into two parties of about ten each and headed out to hunt some Ents.

This Ent they had now discovered was smashed over and over by Basdia's axe and Rita's glaive, its trunk almost completely chopped through. It finally gave a cry like squealing wood and stopped moving.

"Chop it down!" Basdia commanded.

Even the steel wood of the Ents was easier to handle once the monster died. The ghouls cut off the excess branches and wrapped the trunk with ropes so they could transport it.

"Okay! Let's return to the grotto! Phew, I'd really appreciate having Sam here about now."

Dad is helping out Zadilis, Rita said.

Sam and his incredible transportation power had been placed in the same group as Zadilis. Rita's sister Saria joined Vigaro.

"Grrrr?"

"No offense, Skeleton Bear, Skeleton Wolf," Basdia said as the undead whined a little. "You guys are really helping us out."

Without Sam around, the Rotten Beasts mainly handled the job of transporting the defeated Ents. Each of them was already dragging a mighty trunk along. They never got tired, had Brute Strength beyond their beastly powers in life, and understood verbal commands, making them excellent laborers.

I'll carry this one. Basdia, if you and the others can keep an eye on our surroundings. Rita, the Living Bikini Armor, also had the Brute Strength skill.

"Yes, thanks," Basdia said, wiping the sweat from her brow. "We get tired, after all. I'm kinda jealous of you at times like this," Basdia and the other ghouls weren't any weaker than the undead, but they also didn't have the stamina to ceaselessly drag logs around.

We might not get tired, but using battle tech does reduce our MP. I'm jealous of you too, Rita said, looking specifically at Basdia's chest—where sweat was pooling in the deep crevice between her ample mounds. Rita, meanwhile, had absolutely nothing to fill out her own bikini at all.

But of course she didn't. *Enough negativity!* Rita thought. *One day I'll obtain a spirit body, just like my father, and project a sexy body that completely fills this armor out! Winning this Ent hunt is the first step toward that goal! Come on, everyone! Keep moving!*

Rita dragged the log away, with Basdia and the others shouting rowdily as they followed behind her.

"Is that the point of this competition?"

"No, I don't think so."

Basdia and the others had split up to hunt the required

Ents, and things had developed into competing for which group could fell the most. Someone stated that their group would be able to hunt the most, which triggered the whole thing. The ghouls were worried and stressed out about having to flee their home, so this was a great event to alleviate those feelings, and the competition snowballed from there.

"Thinking about it, there's no prizes for winning, nothing lost by losing, and even the rules are pretty vague. But it's perfect for letting off some steam," Basdia said.

"Grrr," the undead agreed.

"Now that the orcs are almost wiped out, there are no enemies left to threaten us," Basdia continued. "The strongest thing in this demon barren is Vandal, followed by Vigaro. With so little danger around, we can afford to have a little fun."

Ents are also fun to hunt, aren't they? agreed Rita. *It's fun to do something different.*

Ents were also an excellent source of materials: not only wood, but their leaves and roots could be used in medicine. Their sap could also be processed into a sweetener. But ghouls had little use for wood as a material, and could only make a limited range of medicines. The sap from the Ents in this particular demon barren wasn't really suited to use as a sweetener either. So the ghouls hadn't bothered hunting Ents previously.

"Normally, the trees right outside the settlement were enough if we needed wood. We didn't need to go looking for Ents. Maybe we'd make shields from them sometimes," Basdia said.

Talea had a lot of Ent wood. Her fan, her throne, she uses it for a lot of things, Rita said.

"I think that's more a matter of personal taste," Basdia said. Ent wood was as hard as steel, which also made it difficult to work with. Even with Talea's skill set, it wasn't easy to perform detailed or delicate work in the medium, or mass-produce items using it. The only one who could basically mold it like clay was Vandal, with his Golem Creation skill.

Basdia and her group took a break in the morning and could see the grotto in the distance by noon. Nothing much happened on the way back, and things were peaceful enough for them to spend most of the time chatting as they moved.

"That's it for Ent hunting, anyway. Although there's probably time for another trip . . ."

But there aren't any Ents to find, Rita said, finishing Basdia's thought for her. Bugogan had already whittled the Ents down before the ghouls came along, and their further deforestation had reduced the number of tree monsters in the barren to practically zero.

If they searched carefully and far afield, they might be able to find a few more Ents of sufficient size. But they basically had enough for the wagons they needed to build.

"Thanks for all your efforts, everyone!" Basdia shouted, punching a fist into the air. "I don't know what the results will be, but we have fought at full strength. That is already worthy of praise!"

Rita and the other ghouls shouted in response. This had been about far more than simply winning or losing.

That said, upon returning to the grotto, Basdia and her team did still want to find out if they were the winners, and so headed toward the designated counting area.

"Welcome back. We'll tally up your haul," said one of the ghouls.

"Two regular-sized logs, and one slightly smaller one, for a total of three. That's not a bad result," Talea said.

The results were also being adjudicated over by Vandal, who had proven himself the strongest in the demon barren. He remained in the grotto to help prepare for the move. Even if he decided to join, his MP Shot was more likely to blow an Ent apart than safely chop it down, so he wasn't really suited to Ent hunting.

Of course, even if he did blow the wood to pieces, he could use his Golem Creation skill to form it back into a single big log. However, if Vandal had joined the contest, everyone would have wanted to be on his team, meaning no contest could have even taken place. Vandal not joining in was another solid indicator of this being a bit of fun for the ghouls.

"Van, are we almost finished?" Basdia asked, looking around the grotto.

The other teams of ghouls, and the cursed carriage that had helped transport the logs, now all seemed to be present. Vigaro and Zadilis were there too.

"Yes, we're done. That should be more than enough, and everyone else has returned," Vandal said.

"You were the last party. If you didn't make it back before noon, we were going to send Skeleton Bird to go look for you," Talea added.

It sounded like totaling up the wood Basdia had just returned with would reveal the winner.

Basdia had just finished telling her group that she didn't care about winning, but in truth, she wanted to win. She took another look around at her rivals, but Vandal had turned all their wood into carriages as soon as it was tallied up, so there was no way to tell how much they had returned with. Vigaro was favored to win and looked confident about it. The other ghouls were nervously waiting for the announcement, now that it was so close, but Vigaro was sitting on the ground, arms crossed, eyes closed, almost as though meditating.

No. Not meditating. Basdia strained her ears for a moment and picked up the sounds of snoring.

"He's asleep?!"

Yes. I tried to stop him, but he was so desperate to win that he dragged three big logs back all on his own, Saria explained. *He used both arms and all of his strength to get them back here.*

Surely, he didn't need to go to quite such lengths. I'm sure your team would have won anyway, Rita replied.

I think he wanted to test out his ranked-up abilities as well. In the end, he practically collapsed there.

"He's like an oversized kid," Basdia mused. Their fearless leader, getting carried away and burning up all his strength.

Mother always used to say that men never grow up, no matter how old they get, Saria said. *What about you, Rita? The Ents kept pretending to be normal trees for us. It was really hard to spot them.*

Ents will do that?! Rita exclaimed.

It seems they will. We threw stones left and right with no response.

"Sounds like they were scared of Vigaro," Basdia said. He was now the second strongest in the jungle demon barren, making him a terrifying foe for rank 3 Ents to consider fighting. They had probably been unaffected by the stones because they were frozen in place by fear.

Interesting. Maybe getting too strong actually has downsides, Rita quipped. Vigaro's party had been forced to work harder, not less, because his strength made the Ents harder to find.

Basdia looked over from Vigaro to the second candidate for first place, her mother, Zadilis. The old ghoul was holding a skewer of meat, and for a moment, Basdia thought she was in the middle of the meal—

"Oh, mother." Basdia shook her head. "Falling asleep while eating. Another child!"

"Huh? Ah! When did I doze off?"

Unlike Vigaro, Zadilis at least had the decency to quickly wake up. She saw her daughter looking down at her with condemnation in her eyes.

"A little nap can't be helped," she said defensively. "I had to use all this magic to take down a single Ent. I had more mages among my group than warriors."

The magic used by Zadilis and the battle tech used by Basdia and the warriors both consumed magical power, but magic drained far more. That was why Zadilis felt like napping, to restore that lost power.

"Everyone! Time to announce the winners!" Talea shouted.

"The end of our time here," Basdia said. "A journey, and a new land at the end of it. I can't wait to start our new lives there." Her heart swelled with both a measure of sadness and soaring expectations for the future.

Incidentally, the victory—as expected—went to Vigaro and his team. But Basdia made a good showing, managing to come in second place.

Afterword

Everyone, thank you for picking up this book. It's nice to meet those of you for whom this is the first time, and welcome back to everyone else. I'm Densuke, the author of this work.

This second book in the series features more characters than Volume 1, and also includes sections that weren't in the online edition, so I hope that you all found it enjoyable. Several characters got to do more than they did in the web novel, so I hope you enjoyed reading their enhanced exploits.

As those who read Volume 1 know, one of the reasons for the main character's bad luck comes down to his name. He was essentially unlucky that someone with a name so similar to his own was on the same ferry.

This also leads me to a source of writing block for me: thinking of names for characters. If there are multiple characters with similar names, I'll end up in a similar position to Rodocolte (one character who didn't even appear in Volume 2). And as this is a work of fantasy, I generally have to think up names using *katakana* letters, rather than also having access to Chinese kanji characters.

I've therefore created a chart of character names. When I bring in a new character, I check over the names of my existing characters to make sure they aren't too similar. On the Earth that the main character originates from, we have two characters who have similar names for story purposes—Hiroto Amamiya and Hiroto Amemiya—but, apart from familial relationships, that would typically be the limit to similar names.

And yet, those of you who have read the web novel already know that yes, I do have more characters with similar names coming up in the future. But this time it wasn't intentional: it was only after posting the story online that my own incorrect use of the names was pointed out to me, and I finally realized what I had done.

In Volume 2, we are yet to encounter these characters with similar names. So why am I bringing this up now? Simply to forewarn you of the appearance of such characters, and to ask for your support in allowing the series to reach a point where this could all happen to begin with!

Well, I'm having a much easier time writing my second afterword! Lastly, allow me to offer some thanks.

To the staff at Hifumishobo and to my editor, who all worked so hard to realize this publication; to Ban! for all the wonderful illustrations; to everyone else involved in this publication; and to my readers, for all their support of *The Death Mage*—thank you all so much! I hope to see you again in the next volume.

—Densuke

Glossary

Aliases
Ghoul King

Regarding Aliases: Aliases can be obtained when people of influence or the general population start using them to refer to an individual. They are also called second names and titles, among other terms. They generally provide bonuses or enhancements to the acquisition or level of skills related to the reasons for acquiring the alias.

Regarding Forced Job Changes: A special kind of punishment used on criminals and slaves. It cannot reduce stats or cause skills to be lost, and the only effect it has on one's status is that the original job will no longer gain levels. However, it is always displayed when checking anyone's stats, which helps to prevent things like slaves escaping. This method was mainly used more than 200 years ago. With developments in alchemy, slave owners nowadays typically force slaves to wear a collar that only the owner can remove.

Characters
Talea

Monsters
Blood Carriage
Black Goblin

Skills

Enhance Brethren

Resist Maladies

Alias: Ghoul King

The Ghoul King alias increases the effects of Enhance Brethren and Death Attribute Allure on ghouls. When Enhance Brethren levels up, it can influence double the number of ghouls.

Talea

Talea is a unique individual: a human girl, blessed with a talent for crafting, while also skilled—not of her own volition—in the arts of the night, and who then underwent the ritual to become a ghoul. She has the males in her group wrapped around her little finger, providing them with weapons and armor while also controlling them with pleasure. Meanwhile, she teaches the other women her wiles and her crafting techniques, placing herself above everyone in the chain of command.

However, she has also never hunted any prey, meaning her level as a monster has never increased, so as a ghoul she is incredibly weak. At the same time, as a crafter, she could easily obtain a noble patron or become the best crafter in a large town. That comes as the result of 200 years of hard work and experience.

Human society could offer her the latest tools, a better working environment, and more varied materials, and if she could change her job back from prostitute to weapons crafter, she would surely be able to further heighten her skills.

Blood Carriage

The carriage version of the Blood Chariot—a war wagon turned into an undead after being embittered by the deaths and grudges of countless fallen warriors. Its wood is stained red with the blood of both enemies and allies. It goes without saying that a normal carriage doesn't tend to experience the number of deaths and grudges required to achieve this feat, and Sam might be the first ever example in Ramda.

Blood Chariots are dangerous undead that only care for killing and running the living over, and will never let people ride inside them even if they have the space. Sam, however, prioritizes transporting people—especially Vandal—and does whatever he can for his passengers' comfort.

His nightly practice of Precision Driving in preparation for the mountain crossing allowed him to acquire the skills Comfortable Handling and Size Control. The spikes and armor added by Talea have also enhanced his combat abilities. Upon ranking up, these additional armaments were fused with the main carriage that is Sam's body.

Black Goblins

A new breed of goblin, created from the fetuses' constant exposure to death attribute magic. Basic rank is 2.

They are a higher form of goblin, with all stats improving upon those of base goblins. They are born with the skills Night Vision, Resist Maladies, and Agility, allowing them to move around at night as though it is daytime, resist poison and sickness, and are fleet of foot. They are also smarter than normal goblins, with an intellect rivaling kobolts, and all of them can be taught to use weapon skills and acquire battle techs with the correct training. In contrast to the twenty-year lifespan of goblins, Black Goblins can hope to live at least double that.

Their sex drive and power to procreate is less than that of regular goblins, however, with lower Breeding and Vigor Drive skills. The young also take longer to reach maturity. When living in a demon barren, goblins become adults a month after being born, while Black Goblins take six months.

They are also bigger than normal goblins and have black skin, as the name suggests. They share some common features with goblins, such as pointed ears and unsettling eyes, but they also have more human features about them. As they have only just appeared as a race, what kind of promoted forms could exist is not yet known. The adventurers' guild would offer a considerable reward for proof that these Black Goblins existed, but such a feat can hardly be considered feasible.

Enhance Brethren

This skill enhances those under the command of the one who possesses it, so long as they are the same race or have some relationship. It can also increase fertility and speed up the development of any children.

The level of the skill changes depending on the number of brethren under the command of the holder. Level 1 is up to 200, level 2 up to 500, and it increases in increments from there.

The races that the Amidd Empire classifies as humans— humanity, elves, and dwarves—cannot learn this skill, but the new races created by Vida can. The majority of those holding this skill are monsters, however, such as Goblin Kings.

Resist Maladies

A skill that allows one to resist not only poison, sickness, and curses, but also anything determined to not be peak physical condition, including exhaustion, stress, tiredness, hunger, suffocation, and pain.

It does not have any influence on MP consumption or injuries taken from damage. Those with this skill at a high level can therefore maintain their peak possible condition even in the worst of circumstances. However, it is a resistance, not nullification, so there are limits to its capabilities.

The skill is generally held by dark elves and the new races created by Vida, such as giantlings, dragonlings, and demonlings, and some monsters. Almost all of them are simply born with it.

It can be leveled up by experiencing a malady, but those who aren't born with it will find it very difficult to acquire. To acquire Resist Maladies, one must experience multiple maladies concurrently. According to records at the adventurers' guild, there are two ways to achieve this. The first is to suffer multiple maladies at the same time, such as poison and sickness, and resist them until the skill takes hold. The second is to learn the resistances to each malady separately, and then wait for them to merge together into the more comprehensive Resist Maladies. Records state that none have managed to survive the first method, and none have achieved the second in a shorter span than ten years.

The effects of the skill Spirit Pollution cannot be mitigated by this skill, or contribute to acquiring it or to leveling it up. This is because the pollution of the spirit is taken as the normal state of existence for the polluted individual.

Densuke

Resides in Saitama Prefecture. Has loved light novels since his childhood and has been writing them himself for close to twenty years. He was aiming to become an author of orthodox fantasy but kept getting distracted along the way. After many twists and turns, he won an award during the Fourth Internet Novel Awards, and achieved his debut as an author. He likes pizza and chicken skin *senbei*, and works out every day. He likes undead heroines the best.

The Death Mage Volume 2
(Yondome ha Iya na Sizokusei Majutusi vol. 2)
© DENSUKE 2017
© BAN! 2017
© HIFUMISHOBO 2017
Originally published in Japan in 2017 by HIFUMISHOBO Co., LTD
English translation rights arranged through TOHAN CORPORATION, TOKYO
.
ISBN: 978-1-64273-243-6

Written by Densuke
Illustrated by Ban!
English Edition Published by One Peace Books 2023

Printed in Canada
1 2 3 4 5 6 7 8 9 10

One Peace Books
43-32 22nd Street STE 204 Long Island City New York 11101
www.onepeacebooks.com